THE FUNDAMENTAL TENDENCY OF OUR TIME

THE WORKS OF EMANUELE SEVERINO

Series editors: Giulio Goggi, Damiano Sacco and Ines Testoni

This book series presents for the first time in the English language the translation of the most important works written by the major twentieth-century Italian philosopher Emanuele Severino. The volumes are translated and edited by scholars and philosophers with an extended knowledge of Severino's theoretical apparatus who provide critical contributions, introductions, and explanatory glosses.

The series publishes Severino's theoretical volumes as well as his more interdisciplinary books, and will be of interest not only to philosophers, but also to readers of cultural and critical theory, the philosophy of religion and the philosophy of science.

Series Editors

Giulio Goggi, Editor of the *Journal of Fundamental Ontology*, and vice-president of ASES (Society for Emanuele Severino Studies)

Damiano Sacco, ICI Berlin, Germany

Ines Testoni, University of Padova, Italy

Other titles in the Series

Beyond Language, Emanuele Severino

Law and Chance, Emanuele Severino

The Originary Structure, Emanuele Severino

THE FUNDAMENTAL TENDENCY OF OUR TIME

On the Technological Destiny of the West

EMANUELE SEVERINO

INTRODUCED AND TRANSLATED BY
ANTIMO LUCARELLI

BLOOMSBURY ACADEMIC
LONDON • NEW YORK • OXFORD • NEW DELHI • SYDNEY

BLOOMSBURY ACADEMIC
Bloomsbury Publishing Plc, 50 Bedford Square, London, WC1B 3DP, UK
Bloomsbury Publishing Inc, 1359 Broadway, New York, NY 10018, USA
Bloomsbury Publishing Ireland, 29 Earlsfort Terrace, Dublin 2, D02 AY28, Ireland

BLOOMSBURY, BLOOMSBURY ACADEMIC and the Diana logo are trademarks of Bloomsbury Publishing Plc

First published in 1981 in Italy as *La tendenza fondamentale del nostro tempo* by Adelphi Edizioni © Adelphi Edizioni S.P.A. Milano, 2008

This book has been translated thanks to a translation grant awarded by the Italian Ministry of Foreign Affairs and International Cooperation.

Questo libro è stato tradotto grazie a un contributo alla traduzione assegnato dal Ministero degli Affari Esteri e della Cooperazione Internazionale italiano.

First published in Great Britain 2026

English language translation © Antimo Lucarelli 2026

Antimo Lucarelli has asserted his right under the Copyright, Designs and Patents Act, 1988, to be identified as Translator of this work.

Copyright @ Giulio Goggi, Daminao Sacco and Ines Testoni 2024

The translation of this book has been realised thanks to a grant awarded by SEPS – SEGRETARIATO EUROPEO PER LE PUBBLICAZIONI SCIENTIFICHE

Via Val d'Aposa 7 - 40123 Bologna
seps@seps.it - www.seps.it

Giulio Goggi, Damiano Sacco and Ines Testoni have asserted their right under the Copyright, Designs and Patents Act, 1988, to be identified as Editors of this work.

Series design: Ben Anslow

Cover image: Italian philosopher, Emanuele Severino / Lido di Venezia, Mostra del Cinema di Venezia 1991. Il filosofo Emanuele Severino; © Marcello Mencarini. All rights reserved 2024.
Contributor: Lebrecht Music & Arts / Alamy

All rights reserved. No part of this publication may be: i) reproduced or transmitted in any form, electronic or mechanical, including photocopying, recording or by means of any information storage or retrieval system without prior permission in writing from the publishers; or ii) used or reproduced in any way for the training, development or operation of artificial intelligence (AI) technologies, including generative AI technologies. The rights holders expressly reserve this publication from the text and data mining exception as per Article 4(3) of the Digital Single Market Directive (EU) 2019/790.

Bloomsbury Publishing Plc does not have any control over, or responsibility for, any third-party websites referred to or in this book. All internet addresses given in this book were correct at the time of going to press. The author and publisher regret any inconvenience caused if addresses have changed or sites have ceased to exist, but can accept no responsibility for any such changes.

A catalogue record for this book is available from the British Library.

A catalogue record for this book is available from the Library of Congress.

ISBN: HB: 978-1-3504-6836-8
PB: 978-1-3504-6835-1
ePDF: 978-1-3504-6838-2
eBook: 978-1-3504-6837-5

Series: The Works of Emanuele Severino

Typeset by Integra Software Services Pvt.Ltd.
Printed and bound in Great Britain

For product safety related questions contact productsafety@bloomsbury.com.

To find out more about our authors and books visit www.bloomsbury.com
and sign up for our newsletters.

CONTENTS

Foreword, Ines Testoni, Damiano Sacco and Giulio Goggi vi

'In technology we trust'
An introduction to Emanuele Severino's understanding of the human technological era,
Antimo Lucarelli 1

Introduction 25

1 About the 'crisis' 33

2 The fundamental tendency of our time and the meaning of the future 45

3 The ethics of science 71

4 Élenchos 89

5 What is Europe? 109

6 Notes on the Italian state of affairs 131

7 Summary: The West as the history of nihilism 155

Notes 173
References 181
Index 182

FOREWORD

Ines Testoni, Damiano Sacco and Giulio Goggi

In the current series, *The Fundamental Tendency of Our Time*[1] marks one of the initial steps in Emanuele Severino's exploration of the role of technics in understanding contemporary Western society and the broader process of Westernization affecting worldwide cultures. This initiative, undertaken as part of Bloomsbury's plan to internationalize the works of the most significant Italian philosopher, advances along two primary tracks. On the one hand, following *The Essence of Nihilism*[2] and *Beyond Language*,[3] the series continues to address Severino's theoretical foundations, which will soon include the publication of his seminal theoretical work: *The Originary Structure*.[4] On the other hand, the second track, initiated with the publication of *Law and Chance*,[5] focuses on observations that in some ways we might call corollaries – in other words, reflections on what appears starting from the radical critique of the error of nihilism. The current volume proceeds along this second track, which will soon expand with further works addressing the theme of the essence of the technoscientific knowledge, including *Téchne: The Roots of Violence, Future Philosophy, The Destiny of Technics*, and *Democracy, Technology, and Capitalism*.[6]

The original of this present book was published a year before the fall of the Berlin Wall; in fact 1988 directly preceded the collapse of Soviet real socialism. It describes a scenario that, until a few years ago, was believed to mark the definitive end of the horrors that characterized the Short Twentieth Century. To historically contextualize the significance of Severino's discussions in this work, it is essential to revisit some of the most historically relevant elements of that period. This approach also highlights how, surprisingly, despite the apparent differences between that time and the present, the issues Severino addresses and the critiques he offers remain remarkably pertinent today.

During the first postwar decades, two opposing blocs were formed with political, military and economic alliances: the Western Bloc (led by the US) defining with NATO a military alliance between the US, Canada and Western European countries, and the Eastern Bloc led by the USSR, around which Eastern European countries gravitated. Thus began what has been referred to as the 'Cold War', namely a global competition that, while not resulting in a direct armed conflict between the two blocs, prevented any kind of cooperation between two parts of the world, with progressive military escalation with the atomic arms race. In the period of operation of such bipolarity at the international level, the Korean and Vietnam Wars developed with polarized positions; the Bay of Pigs Crisis; the wars in Africa and the Middle East; and the space conquest. Although in the 1970s the energy crisis had been accompanied by a period of de-tension with the intention of limiting the exponential growth of nuclear arsenals and dialogues between East and West had begun, in fact the Soviet invasion of Afghanistan played a cooling role in spite of any desire for appeasement, symbolically made explicit by the boycott of the Moscow Olympics by Western countries.

In the 1980s, when *The Fundamental Tendency of Our Time* was written, the loosening of the Cold War polarization became increasingly evident due to the USSR's decline. Mikhail Gorbachev's reforms, *Perestroika* (restructuring) and *Glasnost* (openness), were last-ditch attempts to salvage a collapsing system strained by domestic poverty and the immense economic burden of the arms race. Paradoxically, these reforms further destabilized the Soviet regime, hastening its disintegration. The fall of the Berlin Wall in 1989 symbolically marked the definitive end of bipolar polarization, signifying the collapse of the Soviet Bloc and the emergence of a new world order. This shift was accompanied by the rapid globalization of economies and trade.

During this period, warfare increasingly took the form of guerrilla tactics and, more prominently, terrorism. Both superpowers – seeking to extend or preserve their geopolitical influence – financed and supported armed groups that employed strategies of tension to achieve political objectives. These strategies aimed to instil fear and insecurity among civilian populations, manipulate public opinion, destabilize political systems, and, in some cases, justify the imposition or reinforcement of authoritarian measures.

In Italy, the context in which Severino lived, two opposing extremist forces significantly influenced the sociopolitical climate. On one hand, far-right groups linked to neo-fascism, such as *Ordine Nuovo* (New Order) and *Avanguardia Nazionale* (National Vanguard) along with elements of corrupted secret services, orchestrated attacks aimed at destabilizing the democratic system and paving the way for authoritarian shifts. On the other hand, the *Brigate Rosse* (Red Brigade), whose most infamous act was the 1978 kidnapping and murder of Christian Democratic leader Aldo Moro, were inspired by Soviet Marxism-Leninism and the doctrine of urban guerrilla warfare. Their goal was to overthrow the capitalist system, dismantle the institutions of the bourgeois state, and establish a dictatorship of the proletariat.

The *Partito Comunista Italiano* (PCI) (Italian Communist Party) played a central and multifaceted role during this turbulent period, navigating the US/USSR polarity and the internal debates within international communism concerning Leninism and Stalinism. During the *Anni di Piombo* (Years of Lead), the PCI was the largest communist party in Western Europe and a major political force in Italy. While critical of capitalism, the PCI adopted an autonomous strategy distinct from both the United States and the Soviet Union. It consistently distanced itself from Stalinism, condemning Soviet invasion policies, and under the leadership of Enrico Berlinguer, it championed *Eurocommunism*. This approach rooted itself in parliamentary democracy and European values, marking a shift from traditional Marxist orthodoxy. However, this moderate stance limited the PCI's ability to effectively address the terrorism of the Red Brigades. Its emphasis on reform and democratic processes left it ill-equipped to counteract the violent radicalism of groups like the Brigate Rosse, whose methods and objectives were entirely incompatible with the party's vision for social and political change.

The end of the Cold War, combined with advances in information technology, led to an explosion of international relations and the dismantling of once impassable borders. For a time it appeared that the end of the Cold War represented a definitive turning point in global history, akin to the demise of fascism in the West. However, recent developments in international politics reveal the resurgence of authoritarian and anti-democratic tendencies. Sovereigntist and populist movements, which serve to perpetuate divisions between nations, are fostering attitudes of opposition and rekindling desires to erase identities and differences through the use of military force and invasion strategies. These dynamics challenge the belief that democratic ideologies, with their emphasis on global cooperation and shared perspectives, could sustain a stable and interconnected world order.

Against this critical backdrop, Severino's work continues to demonstrate its timeless relevance. The philosopher, who had already foreseen the collapse of Communism, explicitly announced its inevitability in *The Fundamental Tendency of Our Time*. He attributed this outcome to the intrinsic ethics of technoscience, rooted in the exponential growth of the will to power. This dynamic, according to Severino, ultimately overpowers any other ethical systems, such as those upheld by religions, democracy, or capitalism – ideologies that have historically viewed societal systems and their apparatuses as tools for achieving their respective goals.

The mission of these ideologies has been to seize control of societal systems in their struggle against opposing forces. However, they are ultimately compelled to subordinate their goals to the technoscientific apparatus itself. This dependency sealed the fate of the USSR, which was unable to sustain the unstoppable development of its technoscientific apparatus to compete with the Western Bloc. In any competition where ideologies attempt to use the technoscientific apparatus as a tool to enforce alternative ethical systems, as was the case in the Soviet Union, failure becomes inevitable.

Severino argues that this dominance stems from the nature of technoscientific thinking, understood as the systematic arrangement of means to achieve ends. This mode of thinking represents the ultimate coherence of nihilism – the certainty that being is nothingness, deriving from the belief that being is time and, therefore, that there exists a time when being is not – which underpins the entire tradition of Western thought, including religions and social ideologies. While the West once found meaning in existence through reference to a transcendent, salvific dimension defined as immutable truth guiding ethics and politics, today's nihilistic worldview treats everything as manipulable and available for utilitarian purposes. This shift has led to the autonomous development of the technoscientific apparatus, which no longer serves human wills or ideological aims. Technology has ceased to be merely an instrument; it has become a worldview in itself, grounded in calculation and efficiency. Its internal logic of self-expansion renders traditional systems of meaning obsolete, thereby precipitating a crisis in these structures, which can no longer guide social action.

What unites the period during which Severino was writing this book with the present day are several critical points: no ideology can ignore the necessity of developing technoscientific tools to assert itself over competing ideologies. This establishes the supremacy of technoscience and its apparatus over any ideological system. Consequently, any conflict will be won by those who achieve the highest levels of technoscientific advancement. The fundamental tendency of our time is, precisely, the process as part of which the technoscientific organization of existence is gradually replacing the ideological one.

It should be noted that the technics, of which Severino speaks, is not to be understood in a reductively scientific, physicalistic sense. It is something far more complex: it is the synthesis between the technological potentialities discovered by modern science and the profound essence of contemporary philosophy, which, for the past two centuries, has been showing that there can be no immutable reality that governs the becoming of the world. Separated from that essence, technics is a mere tool in the hands of the forces that intend to use it in order to achieve their goals. United with the essence of the philosophy of our time, technics no longer finds any unsurpassable limits, and imposes itself as the prevailing tool that none of the forces contending for the domination of the world can do without. In this way, however, the end of those forces becomes the infinite increase of the power of technics, which, from a means, becomes the end of every ideology: the servant becomes the master, the master becomes the servant. This is not a 'prophecy', but a 'destiny' that can be grasped by descending into the unconscious of the civilization of the West. But there is an even more radical meaning of 'destiny': it is the gaze that sees the eternity of every being, *qua* being, and the Folly of the faith in the existence of every (ontological) becoming. This is the unprecedented meaning of destiny – that which authentically 'stands' – which is indicated in the pages of *The Fundamental Tendency of Our Time*.

Today, as Severino foresaw, the superpowers include not only the United States and Russia but also China, with India soon to join their ranks. Moreover, the will to power does not equate to a will to self-destruction. Thus, the superpowers – Russia included, due to its maintained nuclear arsenal – are unlikely to engage in direct conflict with each other. Instead, they are more likely to form alliances against weaker nations, particularly those pressing at their borders. This dynamic is evident in issues such as migration and the vulnerability of the world's poorest countries.

All of this remains profoundly relevant today and that is why we believe it is crucial to internationalize this book that demonstrates exceptional predictive capabilities – an aspect that technoscientific knowledge itself would do well to reflect upon, as prediction is precisely its defining strength.

'In technology we trust'

An introduction to Emanuele Severino's understanding of the human technological era

Antimo Lucarelli
*With my thanks to the series editors Ines Testoni,
Giulio Goggi and Damiano Sacco*

1 The quest for innovation and the question of technology. The significance of Severino's philosophy and *The Fundamental Tendency of Our Time*

In the human technological era, *innovation* is an absolute must, as everyone acknowledges. For example, it is a widespread opinion in Europe that if European countries fail to keep up with the innovation pace of the United States and China (communication technologies, military apparatuses, etc.), they will become even more irrelevant on the world stage than they are now. What is *innovation*, though? What is the source of the human capacity to innovate the world? *The Fundamental Tendency of Our Time* by Emanuele Severino, perhaps the greatest Italian thinker of the last century, is a grand philosophical endeavour meant to answer those questions. The present book is the first translation ever published of the Italian original.[1]

In the context of the contemporary quest for it, 'innovation' could be commonsensically defined as 'the development of new products, designs, or ideas'.[2] According to that definition, innovation is especially a *human activity* (though it can also be performed by machines). On the other hand, 'innovation' could also be defined as 'a new idea, design, product', that is as the *effect* of an innovative activity: that is the way in which 'innovation' will be understood in this Introduction.[3] Now, if one were to interpret this definition as a most general one, *literally everything*, which is developed in our times, would be an innovation (and therefore every human activity would be *innovative*). That is why it is more usual to understand 'innovation' (when this is understood as the effect of an innovative activity) in a less general sense. According to that sense, if Apple Inc. started producing their first iPhone again, this 'new' iPhone would not be an *innovation* at all. Indeed, *repetition* is not *innovation*. As a matter of fact, new models of the first iPhone would be 'new' simply due to their being *new copies* of an obsolete model. Yet precisely because of that, even a reproduced old iPhone would prove to be *an innovation*, in that sense.

Thus, the *kind* of innovation, whose pursuit is nowadays acknowledged to be an absolute must, is in fact a *particular kind*: it is the *innovative innovation*, as opposed to innovation *in general*. On the other hand, according to Western thinking, human beings are *in principle* able to produce *something innovative*, such as a new iPhone model, thanks to the *overarching* dimension belonging to all innovations: to the innovative and to the repetitive ones. *This dimension is what Emanuele Severino defines, in more technical philosophical terms, as the ontological dimension of innovation*. Note: not that Severino *agreed* with Western thinking. On the contrary, that is just a diagnosis. A diagnosis *of the 'alienation of the West'* ('alienazione dell'Occidente').[4] Yet in interpreting the Western worldview, Severino detects such an 'ontological' dimension and holds it to be *fundamental* for human action in general, at least according to the culture itself of 'the West' ('l'Occidente'). As a cultural reference, Severino used to recall the definition of 'action' given by Diotima of Mantinea when speaking with Socrates, as per Socrates' own reconstruction – in Plato's *Symposium* (205 BC) – of the conversation he had with Diotima on the essence of 'eros' (ἔρως). In Diotima's definition, every human action is 'poiesis' (ποίησις), that is 'production' of something new. According to Severino, the 'novelty' of the new is here understood by Diotima in its most general sense.

In the present century, *technology* is especially held to be responsible for innovation. Everyone trusts in technology when it comes to producing innovations. In fact, both in philosophy and, more generally, in the cultural reflections of our time, technology is widely agreed to be one defining feature of the present epoch. That is confirmed by Severino's meditation too, though in an original philosophical sense. For him, the present time is the time of the 'civilization of technics' ('civiltà della tecnica'). In that context, given the *innovative* role acknowledged for technology, understanding the meaning of innovation appears to be crucial to understanding *the meaning of technology, and thus the meaning of our epoch*. That is one of the main endeavours of *The Fundamental Tendency of Our Time*. In this Introduction, I will sketch an overview of the central considerations made by Emanuele Severino in this book and clarify their most difficult aspects.

2 The invention of ontological innovations. Ancient Greek philosophy in Severino's interpretation

Predictably, a philosophical meditation on innovation *redefines* the terms of the matter. That is true now and was true more than two thousand years ago, when philosophy was born. Indeed, philosophy began to meditate on the ontological meaning of innovation from when philosophy was born. Yet according to Severino's interpretation, philosophy has not only *launched the meditation* on ontological innovation: *philosophy has launched innovation itself*. That is to say that it was Ancient Greek philosophy that started conceiving of innovation *in the way in which*, progressively over the course of the West's (and of the world's) history, innovation has been generally understood.[5] To put in another way, innovation is *a philosophical invention* (leaving aside, for now, whether this invention was a discovery or a fabrication of philosophers). However, that is not to say that philosophical theories (allegedly the kind of 'product' which philosophy is able to invent) are the most valuable and innovative of all innovations. On the contrary, it is to say that philosophy has invented inventing itself: philosophy has historically been the inventor of inventors. And given the ineliminable role that innovations have played in Western history, philosophy, as Severino argues, has established *Western culture itself*. How is that possible, though? Is it not *counterintuitive* to argue that philosophy has established the Western worldview and common sense, rather than common sense philosophy?

As I have started to show, the answer to these questions is grounded in the *general*, that is *ontological* dimension of innovation. In the last section, I have alluded to that dimension by recalling the *commonsensical distinction* between repetitive and innovative innovations. In truth, I believe it is general understanding that even mere repetitions are a sort of innovation, in that *innovating*, in its most general sense, simply means *producing something new*. According to this sense, *everybody invents, and everybody innovates*: Philosophies are 'inventions' of philosophers, technologies are 'inventions' of technologists.

As hidden as it may be, the most *general* sense of innovation has an *ontological* core. Historically speaking, *ontology* is the discourse on *being*. In Severino's reconstruction of the Western worldview (a perfectly traditional reconstruction, as acknowledged by Severino himself), the ontological component of innovating lies in *bringing something new to existence*. Therefore, innovation 'innovates' in that it brings to existence something which did not exist before, even if this is just a new copy of the first iPhone model. Indeed, even a *new old iPhone* is *new*, for it can be genuinely brought to existence and thus represents an *innovation in being*. An *ontological innovation*. Even after the fabrication of the *n*th new old iPhone, reality is *richer, newer* than it used to be: in philosophical terms, *being* is richer, newer than it used to be. Now, this fundamental *ontological effect* of innovating is defined by Severino as 'ontological becoming' ('divenire ontologico'). That is the meaning itself of *ontological innovation*.

According to Severino's reconstruction, ontological becoming was introduced by Ancient Greek philosophers. These philosophers have not simply brought to light what had been unconsciously present in the pre-ontological and pre-philosophical worldview: Rather, they have *established* ontological becoming. Therefore, *before* Ancient Greek philosophy was born (to then colonize, over the centuries, the culture of the entire world), things did not *begin* to exist, if 'beginning' means 'innovation in being'. Before Ancient Greek philosophy, the *origin* of things that presented themselves in experience, such as the sky, the earth, and humans themselves, was not yet identified with *that from which* something needs to come for it to be a genuine novelty. That is to say that the origin of things was not yet identified with *nothingness*. Before Ancient Greek philosophy, humans, the earth, and the sky might even have *always existed*, and therefore, they were not understood as having an *origin*, a *beginning*, in the sense which was then introduced. Thus, *in the pre-philosophical and pre-ontological world*, there existed no *innovation*, understood as it is nowadays. That is Severino's reconstruction.

On the other hand, this reconstruction does not rule out the fact that *a different sense of 'novelty'* marked the world perceived by pre-philosophical humanity. Severino accounts for that fact by distinguishing *ontological becoming* from *pre-ontological becoming* ('divenire pre-ontologico'). Let me give an example. In the pre-Ancient-Greek world, a rough stone made into a spear tip represented a kind of *innovation* in that the stone became something *else* than it was. *Pre-ontological* innovation. Yet speaking rigorously, *this* 'novelty' of the spear tip includes nothing *innovative*: After all, what is there new in the spear tip? *Any answer to that question must presuppose the ontological component of innovation*, that is *ontological becoming*. For the spear tip can be considered *new*, compared to the stone wherefrom it was fashioned, *if it is seen as a previously non-existing entity*. This suggests that whereas the *ontological kind* of innovation deserves to be called *innovation*, the *non-ontological kind* would perhaps better be defined as *pre-ontological becoming*. That is what Severino does.

In conclusion, the pre-philosophical world was marked by a *pre-ontological understanding* of innovation, whereas with regards to ontological innovations, it is Severino's opinion that these clearly emerged with Ancient Greek philosophy. At most, Severino is ready to concede that it is *unclear* whether, further to the pre-ontological understanding of becoming, the pre-philosophical humanity already conceived of becoming in an ontological fashion. In other words, Severino is ready to concede that from an ontological perspective, the origin and the destiny of things in the pre-philosophical worldview *retain an ambiguous character*: one cannot be sure whether the spear tip was thought to come from nothingness or to have always existed.

3 Traditional Western metaphysics as a means to predict (and nullify) ontological innovations

When appearing on history's stage, Ancient Greek philosophy not only establishes the ontological dimension of innovation. In Severino's interpretation, philosophy feels threatened by the very 'danger' ('pericolo') it has evoked – the danger posed by the possibility to create and destroy. Thus, philosophy evokes *at the same time* the 'remedy' ('rimedio') against the danger: Philosophy becomes *metaphysics*. From a descriptive perspective, Severino's notion of 'metaphysics' is perfectly traditional, yet from an evaluative perspective, 'metaphysics' is to be considered for him 'the extreme form of human alienation' ('la forma estrema dell'alienazione dell'uomo'). In this Introduction, I will focus mainly on the descriptive aspect.[6] According to Severino, 'metaphysics' was born as the establishment of a 'Meaning' ('Senso') of the world: The effect of this was that all ontological novelties *could be anticipated* with regards to their 'Meaning', or 'essence'.[7] That is Severino's peculiar explanation for the fact that philosophy was born as a meditation concerned with *essences*. As I will show, the establishment of a Meaning of reality is *something shared* by both traditional and anti-traditional metaphysics, though there are deep differences between the two. In this context, let me conclude by noting that for Severino, *simultaneously*, philosophy was born by creating the danger and the remedy against the danger. That is the peculiar essence of philosophy as *traditional metaphysics*.

Now, what is the 'remedy'? What the 'danger'? The danger is the very world established with the establishment of ontological innovations: a world where the origin and the destiny of things is *nothingness*. Even today, technological actors on the world stage *can* innovate *because* the product of their innovative activity *emerges from nothing*, that is, from its *absolute nonexistence*. It emerges *ex nihilo sui*. On the other hand, the remedy for the danger is the *Meaning* discovered by a *novel kind of knowledge*, later called *metaphysics*. Its principal activity lies in detecting and establishing a Meaning of the world, thanks to which the *absolute novelty* of ontological innovations can be *tamed*. That is, *predicted*. Let me explain.

Itself an innovation brought forth by Ancient Greek philosophy, metaphysical knowledge is a very peculiar kind of knowledge. It embraces all times, all spaces, and identifies their Meaning. In other words, the Meaning of the world is the Meaning *of all that is*, whenever and wherever this is. Yet according to Severino's analysis, the Meaning discovered by metaphysical knowledge, being capable of embracing all times, *captures* the essence of the future *ahead of time*. Accordingly, the knowledge of this Meaning, i.e. the metaphysical knowledge, becomes able to genuinely *foreknow* the future, no matter how *unpredictable* this can be. Let me give an example. Assuming that one possesses the *metaphysical certainty* that the Meaning of the world resides in its being created by God, meaning that *absolutely everything* is created by God, one can *foresee* that whatever the future brings, that will be *ens creatum*. Nowadays, Christianity is of course a perfect example of this metaphysical view.

However, being able to foresee what the future will be like means being able to *predict* all possible novelties, even though simply with regards to their essential 'Meaning'. Now, can a *predictable novelty* preserve its *ontological* character? Can *that*, which arises from nothingness, be anticipated with a prediction? The answer is a negative one. According to Severino's interpretation of the development of Western thinking, *traditional metaphysics* ends up *preventing the possibility* of innovations *in being* – the very metaphysics that *invented* those innovations. In Severino's reconstruction, the crucial criticism made by *anti-traditional* metaphysics against traditional metaphysics is that *if* there exists a Meaning of the world, the origin (and the destiny) of things is not *nothingness* anymore. If one can predict *what* the future will be like, even though simply with regards to its Meaning, the future is not *the future* anymore. For 'the future' is nothingness itself. That is simply the *Western* notion of 'future', according to Severino. But *nothingness* cannot be *pre-determined* by any anticipatory knowledge.

Nonetheless, that is the impossible task which Western metaphysics originally assigned to itself: the 'entification of nothingness' ('entificazione del niente'), as per Severino's terminology.[8] By attempting to predict the future (that is, nothingness), traditional Western metaphysics has *entified* it. It has turned nothingness into *being*. Therefore, the unprecedented contribution of Ancient Greek metaphysics to the world's history, i.e. *the possibility to innovate the world*, is contradicted by Ancient Greek metaphysics itself: since its very beginnings, metaphysics is at war with itself.[9]

Let me note that Severino primarily conceives of 'entification' as an *intrinsically metaphysical* attempt. That is to say that all those predictions not predicting the world *with regards to its Meaning* are not *entifications*. Therefore, the 'peccatum originale occidentale' lies in the attempt to foresee what had been originally conceived as unpredictable *from a metaphysical perspective*. That is why I mentioned that Severino's reconstruction of the history of Western metaphysics is perfectly traditional: the attempt to detect a Meaning in reality failed, for reality is too immense to be captured by any Meaning. Mutatis mutandis, one can here compare Severino's interpretation to Martin Heidegger's, but more generally to contemporary anti-metaphysics (broadly conceived).

4 Anti-traditional metaphysics as a means to predict (and preserve) ontological innovations

We are now closer to the question of technology: This question will transform into the question of 'technics' ('tecnica'), for reasons that will soon become clear. Yet in order to come to that question, the criticism made by anti-traditional metaphysics against traditional metaphysics needs to be investigated further. In this context, anti-traditional metaphysics will appear as *the essential condition for the historical birth of 'technics'*. Indeed, in Severino's opinion, the crucial moment in the entire history of the West is the acknowledgement of the fact that ontological becoming *has been rendered inconceivable* by the very metaphysics that established it, and that therefore, even the *innovative power of human actions* has been made inconceivable. It is with this acknowledgement, which according to Severino first occurred in the nineteenth century thanks to Giacomo Leopardi (and then, to Friedrich Nietzsche and Giovanni Gentile), that the Western history was divided into two fundamental epochs, *more fundamentally different from each other* than any epoch from any other: The anti-traditional and the traditional epoch.[10]

Now, as has been stated, it is because of its claim to be able to detect the Meaning of the world that Western metaphysics ended up nullifying innovation. As a matter of fact, *if traditional metaphysics were right*, innovations (i.e. metaphysical innovations) would not be possible. Yet innovation happens all the time. Not that traditional metaphysics did not deem innovation possible, *sic et simpliciter*. Rather, it deluded itself into thinking that a Meaning of the world could *coexist* with the world's *becoming*, understood as a metaphysical becoming. Therefore, the dismissal of the ancient metaphysical claim is the *condition* for anti-traditional metaphysics to *preserve* the possibility to innovate, that is the dimension of *ontological becoming*. Even better, *the only metaphysical claim which anti-traditional metaphysics can advance is that no metaphysics is possible*. For the Meaning of being is the absence itself of a Meaning. That is, *it is the presence of novelty, of innovation, of becoming*, which require, in order to exist, the nonexistence of Meaning. However, that is not to say that anti-traditional metaphysics is inconsistent. On the contrary, it is *in order to be consistent* with its faith in the existence of ontological becoming that metaphysics becomes, over the course of Western history, a metaphysics of novelty. Thus, according to Severino's reconstruction of the history of philosophy, in order to preserve novelty, metaphysics had to become, *sic et simpliciter*, a metaphysics of novelty.[11]

Yet, does that mean that *predictions* are no longer possible? That would be counterintuitive. In effect, is it not evident that the power of prediction has *increased* thanks to the emergence of modern science and its technologies? Are we not able to control things much better than we could in the past, even the recent past? Yet how can predictions still be made, if *predicting itself* nullifies the future?

These questions give me the chance to provide some clarifications. For Severino, it is primarily the *metaphysical* prediction that nullifies the future, not *every* prediction. This entails that the only way to predict the essence of innovations is to predict them as *essentially unpredictable*. Therefore, nowadays, one can *predict* that every course of events is essentially unpredictable, that is unpredictable *with regards to its Meaning*. In that sense, for Severino, human beings are of course still able to make predictions. Indeed, it is precisely *because of the acknowledgement that all human predictions predict the unpredictable*, that one can nowadays make predictions. Once, these predictions were thought to be *incontrovertible*, at least when they were *metaphysical* predictions (and metaphysical predictions were not only in the minds of metaphysicians). Today, on the contrary, predictions *explicitly recognize themselves as fallible*. They acknowledge (or are destined to acknowledge according to Severino) to be *always fallible*. That happens because the true incontrovertible prediction, i.e. the prediction not able to be contradicted by the facts, could only be the metaphysical one. Nowadays, predictions attempt to predict the unpredictable itself. After all, that is the very root of the anxiety of contemporary man: A new, immense anxiety.

5 On 'technics'. Terminological remarks

We are now ready to approach the question of 'technics'. I will first make some terminological considerations. In the translation published in this book, I have chosen to translate the word *tecnica*, used by Severino, with 'technics', following the choice made by Damiano Sacco in his translations of Severino for the present Bloomsbury series.[12] Yet the word *tecnica* may also be translated into 'technology'. So far, in this Introduction, I have been intentionally confusing them. Nonetheless Sacco's choice presents the advantage of keeping *tecnica* and *tecnologia* distinct: indeed, using the word *technology* to translate both these Italian words could create confusions. Furthermore, choosing the English word *technique* to translate 'tecnica', which would be the most natural choice, would presumably be inconvenient because of the difficulty to make *technique* allude to the essential dimension of *all techniques*. That is what Severino refers to when speaking of 'technics', as I will show.

On the other hand, it must be acknowledged that there is no specific English adjective for the noun *technics*: In fact, 'technical' refers to 'technique', even when one speaks of a 'technical term', a 'technical question', a 'technical remark'. These are all 'technical' in that they are inspired by a certain technique (the different fields of human knowledge are themselves 'techniques'). Therefore, one is forced to use the adjective *technological* even when this does not refer to *technology*. This happens in Severino's Italian too, though: at times, Severino uses the adjective *tecnologico* to refer to *tecnica* ('technics'), although *tecnologico* usually alludes to the *commonsensical* acceptation of 'tecnica' (analogous to the English *technique*). That is part of why Severino happens to use also *tecnico* ('technical') to refer to *tecnica* ('technics'). For these reasons, I have followed Sacco's translation. Another reason, even though of a different kind, is of course represented by the helpfulness of the consistency between translations for the reader.

6 Unpredictability as the driver of power: technics as the 'will to increase power indefinitely'

Let me come to the question of 'technics'. As for Martin Heidegger, so in Emanuele Severino, *technics* is not a tool that modern science has been able to manufacture, such as iPhones, missiles or nuclear weapons. That is to say that both for Severino and for Heidegger, technics is *a human way of being* (at least thus far). Combining two Latin nouns, one could say that 'technics' is simply the *homo technicus*. Yet nowadays, humanity usually conceives of technics as something which is *other than itself*. One should not be surprised, though, for as Heidegger argued, humanity conceives of technics (*Technik*, in German) as a human tool because that is how humanity *hides from itself its being a tool of technics*. Indeed, 'technics' appears to be the dominant way of being human in the contemporary age.[13] Yet what is technics for Severino, finally?

To answer that question, we need to go back to predictions. As a matter of fact, the first consequence of the impossibility of incontrovertible (that is, metaphysical) predictions is that the human capacity to predict the future becomes *essentially more powerful*. After all, it is common experience that if one does not trust one's own capacity to predict the future, one enhances one's efforts to make the prediction as trustable as it can be. That is, one enhances one's efforts to control reality as much as one can. An entirely new attitude towards the future is therefore embedded, for Severino, in the human technological era. The fact that there is no Meaning that *limits* the human capacity to foresee the future, that is *the human capacity to control reality*, entails that there is no limit to human will and actions.

By bringing to light the inconsistency of all attempts to identify a Meaning of reality, anti-traditional metaphysics has brought to light the inconsistency of *all limits* which could be *imposed* on reality. Indeed, by definition, the Meaning *limits* the possibilities of reality: Let us take think again of Christian metaphysics. From the Christian-metaphysical perspective, it belongs to the Meaning of things that human action cannot affect humans' biological life, as this is only possible to God, *just as any other 'action'*: God is the only true actor, for without God, no action whatsoever can have its effect. That makes the Christian Meaning of reality, given by the fact that everything is caused by God, a *limit* to reality's possibilities. Yet *now* that Western metaphysics realized that limits are just lies, Western peoples start both willing and acting in order to make the 'impossible' happen.

Let me note that the impossibility of *metaphysical* limits, discovered by anti-traditional metaphysics, does not entail for Severino that even *empirical* limits vanish. For example, if humanity had not already discovered the technology to affect human biological life, this technology would have not become possible simply thanks to the acknowledgement that the metaphysical limits have been falsely imposed on reality by the Western tradition. *However is an empirical limit a true limit?* As a matter of fact, a metaphysical limit is such that in no case it can be broken. In other words, the metaphysical limit has the modal character of necessity. On the contrary, a *non-metaphysical limit*, that is an *empirical* limit, no matter how unsurpassable, is *contingent*: it is a limit which *can* be broken. Therefore, no matter how extraordinary the conditions required to break the limit, and no matter whether the limit will eventually be broken or not, a contingent limit *can in principle* be broken. Now, does that not mean that all contingent limits are not limits *in the strictest sense*?

If the 'limit' is *to limit*, without the possibility to be broken, the only real limits to reality should be considered to be the *metaphysical limits*, for they can never be broken, no matter how advanced the technological progress of humanity can become. But in an era where metaphysical limits have been shown to be illusory, *there is no limit to the innovation humans can achieve*, for there is no limit to what the world can be. *It is exactly this omnipotent will*, resulting from the awareness of such an absence of limits, *that Emanuele Severino calls 'technics'*. Thinking of this will, one can understand why the *technological being* is nowadays represented by the *homo technicus*. That is going to stay true until another being that is capable of will takes the place of humans, *if* that will ever happen.

Let me briefly note that I am using a twofold notion of power here. Indeed, *in a mere psychological sense*, power is the power one is convicted to have. In that sense, according to the Severinian definition of 'technics', the power of technics simply lies in the *conviction* that the technological will has to have boundless capacities. Nevertheless, one cannot reduce power to a *psychological conviction*. For the boundless will of 'technics' can show the successes it has achieved, i.e. the technologies it has produced. After all, 'technics' has proved to be able to break the unbreakable. For example, walking on the moon or destroying humanity with a couple of bombs were genuinely thought to be impossible things, before 'technics' came. That means that there is also a *real* dimension to power. *Power is therefore made up of psychological and real power*.

Nonetheless, Severino's considerations in *The Fundamental Tendency of Our Time* are going to show that even real power is *unreal*. That is due to its belonging to the *alienation of Western culture*. However, in order for the reader to fully understand this judgement by Severino, a more thorough discussion of his philosophy of 'technics' is required, especially with regards to the extent and the modalities in which technics exerts its power. I will devote the rest of this Introduction to this matter.[14]

7 Never just a tool: technics and technology

For Severino, 'technics' is the *alleged* omnipotent will that has been making all *technological* products possible. In other words, it is only because humans *became*, at a certain time in history, *technological*, that any kind of *technology* could be produced. This definition of the *technological tool* follows from Severino's notion of 'technics'. According to that definition, technology is never *just* a tool, such as a nuclear weapon, a missile or an iPhone. Not that *technology* is a human way of being, though. Indeed, that is the meaning of *technics*. Technology is never just a tool in the sense that it is *always a tool encountered by humans*. And humans change, according to the epoch. And when humans change, *their tools change*. That is not to say that, say, a satellite in low Earth orbit, similar to the thousands launched by SpaceX, would have been *possible* in the Ancient Greek world. It is to say, though, that the satellite would have been impossible *not simply because the Ancient Greeks had not yet achieved the current level of technological progress*. The satellite would have *also* been impossible *because the Ancient Greeks would have not looked at it as technological humans do in the technological era*. Indeed, the satellite would not have represented *the product of the boundless capacities of human will and action*. That is because human will was not thought to have boundless capacities. Even a satellite is never just a set of components.

8 The extent of the technological power

In the last sections, I have recalled Severino's notion of *technics*. This has proved to be the will to push back limits that are still existing and opposed by human will. Technics has been *empowered* by the metaphysical discovery that there are no real limits, but merely empirical ones: limits *de facto*, not *de jure*. That is why Severino claims that *philosophy has made technics and technology possible*.

Now, the *context* where Severino collocates technics is the conflict between the great forces of our time: economic forces, such as capitalism; political-institutional forces, such as democracies; religious forces for Severino, such as Christianity. Such forces can also be distinguished with regards to the degree of advancement of their metaphysical worldview. In that sense, for Severino forces are divided into *traditional forces*, still marked by a (traditional) metaphysical worldview, and *anti-traditional forces*, whose only metaphysics is the metaphysics of innovation. As examples, one can think, respectively, of Christianity and of contemporary atheism (keeping in mind that atheism, to be genuinely anti-traditional, should not see in the nonexistence of God just another Meaning of reality). Within this frame, it is Severino's opinion that technics, *on the one hand*, is one of the conflicting forces, *and on the other*, is the *tool* that all forces are increasingly employing in order to win the battle against the others for the realization of their respective purposes. That is not to say that technics is a *physical entity* employed as a tool by those forces: only technology can be a tool in that sense. Rather, technics is *the means* which all forces of our age are using to achieve their goals. In other words, Christians, citizens of democracies and capitalists are acquiring *a certain way of being*: the technological way of being. What does that mean, more concretely?

According to Severino, *even technology* is increasingly being employed by contemporary forces, though in a merely instrumental sense. In effect, Severino argues that *all* forces of our world are using *technology too* as a tool (let us recall that technology is not just a tool: it is the product of technological action and will). In his oral speeches, he used to exemplify this by referring to the fact that the Holy See has one of the most advanced apparatuses of communication technologies of our time. Similar statements by Severino allude to the *system of physical tools* that modern science has made possible, such as the internet, satellites, submarines. Now, it is Severino's opinion that *even traditional forces*, still marked by a (traditional) metaphysical view of reality, *are increasingly employing modern technology to be able to better realize their purposes*.

Therefore, just as *technology* is being used by all contemporary forces (traditional and anti-traditional ones), it is Severino's view that technics too is being used by those forces as a tool. A new tool, marked by an immense power. That holds even though, in a strict sense, a *traditional* force could never use technics as a tool, for that would mean to lose its nature. For instance, how could Christianity become *technological* and thus share the idea of there being no true limits to human will? When stating that *even technics* is a tool increasingly utilized by contemporary forces, Severino means that *what has been made possible by technics*, that is, *modern technology*, is being utilized, *in a merely instrumental sense*, by all forces to increase their power. After all, employing a system of communications technology does in no way oblige one to adopt the *technological will* that produced it.

9 A peculiar case of modernization of traditional forces: on technological democracy

If on one hand, all traditional forces are more and more resorting to technics (in the instrumental sense just mentioned) to realize their goals, on the other hand, some traditional forces are abandoning their nature to assume a *secularized form*: In other words, they are converting to *technological forces*. Here, I will sketch an overview of this process with regards to *democracy* as one of the core political-institutional forces of the contemporary age.

Nowadays, one can observe that forces that are willing to modernize themselves are able to *better realize* the Meaning they once thought was already realized by the very nature of things. Democracy is one of them. As a matter of fact, in the contemporary age, new wars and generally worsening conditions of life are forcing more and more democratic citizens to acknowledge that *democracy is in peril*. Yet *if* democracy is in peril, that means democracy cannot be the ultimate political acquisition of civilized humanity, as many democratic citizens thought in the past. In other words, democracy *as Meaning*, i.e. as an absolutely ineliminable element of reality, has fallen. As paradoxical as it may sound, *it is exactly to preserve democracy that the democracies of our time seem to be abandoning the idea that the democratic form of state is a definitive acquisition of human history*. After all, it is a common opinion that *the less one takes democracy for granted, the safer democracy is*.

According to Severino, the process of modernization is no *instrumental transformation*. It is not because democracy wants to keep itself safe that it has abandoned the idea of its historical finality. On the contrary, it is because democracy *lost its certainty* in the truth of this finality that democracy *can*, as a *technological* democracy, *attempt* to preserve itself in the technological world. That is the essence of *technological democracy*. In other words, it is not because they have never been really interested in the *truth* of their metaphysical views that forces, such as democracy, are changing. In that respect, Severino's reading is radically different from, say, Friedrich Nietzsche's reading. According to Nietzsche, the hidden ground of Western metaphysics is represented by the *will to power*, that is, *not* by a genuine theoretical intent. On the contrary, Severino is among the thinkers who take seriously the Western metaphysical endeavour. *Yet on the other hand*, even for him, *albeit, in a different sense*, the hidden fundament of Western metaphysics, both the traditional and the anti-traditional one, is the 'will to power' ('volontà di potenza'). In this context, let me remind that in any case, when it comes to interpreting the history of Western metaphysics, it is important to acknowledge what is at stake: an interpretation of the history of Western culture cannot be *incontrovertibly* demonstrated. That is Severino's opinion too. When it comes to reconstructing history, it is just a matter of interpretation. That is, *of faith* – a faith which, like contemporary forces, always fights with its opposite faiths.[15]

10 The rebellion of the tool: technics and contemporary forces as its tools

That is not the end of Severino's meditation on technics. For according to the Severian reading, technics is destined to rebel against all forces which are using it and to become *itself the user of these forces*: the forces are destined to become the tool of their tool. In fact that is *The Fundamental Tendency of Our Time*.[16] According to Severino, all forces of our era are *moving their respective goals to the background* in order to pursue the *technological goal*. In that context, the conflict among forces becomes 'a secondary clash' ('uno scontro di retroguardia').[17]

Severino does not mean that technics, understood as the omnipotent will empowered by anti-traditional metaphysics, is becoming *itself the goal* of other forces. Indeed, technics is the *condition* of all forces. In other words, an omnipotent will is not itself *a concrete will*, for it lacks concrete content, that is a concrete goal. It is generic *by nature*. After all, *what* is one going to do with this omnipotent will? That question stays unanswered until a *concrete content* is determined by this will, in order for this to *will* it. In that sense, technics can certainly not *become autonomous* and give itself content. An analogous discourse should be made with regards to *another* feature of technics, as per how this is understood by Severino, which I have not mentioned so far. I am alluding to the fact that technics wants to indefinitely increase its power *also in a different sense* than the one which I clarified in this Introduction.[18] For Severino, technics also wants to indefinitely increase its *capacity to realize purposes* ('capacità di produrre scopi'). Even this will is a *generic* one, though. Therefore, one should not interpret Severino as stating that an *autonomous* technological will is possible. What then does he mean?

Severino's thesis is that *in pursuing their own purposes*, all contemporary forces start using *what has been made possible by technics:* that becomes the *pre-eminent goal* which makes the forces' goals secondary. Indeed, in pursuing one's purpose, one can be *eased* by an (alleged) omnipotent will not because this gives one *one's purpose*, but because it gives one *the condition for the realization* of one's purpose. If one believes oneself to be the only creator of one's inventions, with all due respect to God, it is certainly *on the basis of a will without limits*, and particularly without the limit represented by the necessary contribution of God to one's inventions, that one can intend to realize their personal purposes. *On that technological basis*, one can will whatever one wants to will. For instance, one can will to create a multiplanetary humanity.

Therefore, it is *in this sense* that technics can become one's pre-eminent purpose and subjugate one's specific purposes: not in the sense that it becomes *a purpose among purposes*, but in the sense that it becomes the condition of all purposes. *In this sense*, one's purpose becomes secondary, instrumental, as opposed to the situation where one's purposes are not mediated by the technological purpose in any way and are therefore *non-technological* purposes.

An analogous discourse should be made, as I mentioned, with regards to technics as the will to indefinitely increase the *capacity to realize purposes*. Indeed, one can never pursue a *generic* enhancement of one's capacity to realize purposes: it is always a *specific actor* who pursues the enhancement. For instance, a *military* actor as the Pentagon is going to pursue a *military enhancement* of its capacities. Only, the Pentagon is going to do that *in a technological way*, that is by assuming that there is no limit to the extent of its capacity to realize its purposes: The extent is *indefinite*.

11 The necessity to actualize certain considerations by Severino in *The Fundamental Tendency of Our Time*

Before concluding this Introduction, let me note that certain considerations by Severino, where he shows how technics actualizes in the world's geopolitical scenario, need to be actualized. One can take Severino's remarks on the 'USA-USSR duumvirate' as an example. Indeed, just as the Italian Communist Party (PCI), the 'Union of Soviet Socialist Republics' does not exist anymore.[19] Now, in 1988, when *The Fundamental Tendency of Our Time* was published, Severino detected the pre-eminence of technics as actualized in the so-called 'USA-USSR duumvirate': According to him, both these two geopolitical actors had moved to the background their respective political purposes and were both pursuing them in a technological fashion. What is left nowadays of such 'duumvirate', though?

Answering that question entails embracing Severino's perspective and making it 'speak' as Severino would have spoken. That being said, I believe that *on one hand*, the USA and Russia are still to be considered, from a

Severinian perspective, the two principal geopolitical actors on the world stage, given their incomparable nuclear power: that was Severino's opinion itself after he spectated the dissolution of the Soviet Union. *On the other hand*, even if it is true that other actors, such as China, are progressively replacing Russia on the world's stage, that simply means that technics is being increasingly and better utilized by these actors rather than Russia. For example, that is to say that China is optimizing its development and usage of technologies made possible by technics: China is the new Russia. Therefore, I believe Severino's general discourse stays unchanged, even if it is actualized in another historical scenario.

12 Conclusion

In conclusion, let me briefly summarize the overview of Severino's philosophy of technics which I have given. For Severino, technics is *the will that believes that there are no limits to reality, and therefore, no limits to human will, the extent of whose power is indefinitely increasable.* In that context, *The Fundamental Tendency of Our Time* is the tendency according to which *all forces in our age start resorting to the technological tools made possible by modern science thanks to a technological will.* This becomes the fundamental purpose of those forces: it becomes the purpose of their purposes.

– Montefalcone di Val Fortore, Italy, 26th January 2025

Bibliography

Cusano, Nicoletta. 2011. *Emanuele Severino. Oltre il nichilismo*. Brescia: Morcelliana.
Goggi, Giulio. 2015. *Emanuele Severino*. Vatican City: Lateran University Press.

Lucarelli, Antimo. 2021. *Per un nuovo concetto di fenomeno: Muovendo da Heidegger e Severino*. Soveria Mannelli: Rubbettino.
Lucarelli, Antimo. 2025. 'Is metaphysics totalitarian? First remarks on politics and metaphysics in Emanuele Severino'. In: *Italian Thought*, edited by F. Dal Bo and C. Salzani. New York: SUNY Press, pp. 97–117.
Severino, Emanuele. 1980. *Destino della necessità. Κατὰ τὸ χρεών*. Milan: Adelphi.
Severino, Emanuele. 1981. *La struttura originaria*. Milan: Adelphi.
Severino, Emanuele. 1988. *La tendenza fondamentale del nostro tempo*. Milan: Adelphi.
Severino, Emanuele. 2006. *Cosa arcana e stupenda*. Milan: BUR Rizzoli.
Severino, Emanuele. 2015. *In viaggio con Leopardi: La partita sul destino dell'uomo*. Milan: BUR Rizzoli.
Severino, Emanuele. 2021. *Il nulla e la poesia*. Milan: BUR Rizzoli.
Severino, Emanuele. 2023. *Beyond Language*. Translated by Damiano Sacco, edited by Giulio Goggi, Damiano Sacco, and Ines Testoni. London: Bloomsbury Academic.
Severino, Emanuele. 2023. *Law and Chance*. Translated by Damiano Sacco, edited by Giulio Goggi, Damiano Sacco, and Iines Testoni. London: Bloomsbury Academic.

Introduction

One wonders what Europe's legacy in the world is. Generally, one leaves a legacy when one dies. In what sense is Europe unequivocally dead? In the sense that it does not dominate the world anymore. Europe has left this task to the United States and to the Soviet Union, or better, to the Superstate ['Superstato', t/n] emerging from the *concordia discors* of those two superpowers. The fate of the Earth now 'ultimately' depends on the USA–USSR Duumvirate. However, the planetary duumvirate has inherited from Europe the principle of the collegial leadership of the world, which the European hegemonic nations implemented until the First World War.

Yet, if we are to understand what is occurring on Earth today, we are inevitably pushed backwards, into the remote past of our history: we are pushed to the origins of the European civilization. The effectiveness of the leadership of the world exerted by the USA–USSR Duumvirate is due to the level of development reached by the technological Apparatus. However, the technics ['tecnica', t/n] of our time is inconceivable without modern science. We can hope to discover where technics is taking us only if we find out where science is taking us. But likewise, modern science is inconceivable without Ancient Greek philosophy. We can discover where science is taking us only if we manage to discern the space where Ancient Greek philosophy has taken Europe.

In general, one is willing to step back from technics to science; nonetheless, one is much less willing to step back from science to philosophy, and specifically to Ancient Greek philosophy. On the pretence of science being born from a break with the philosophical tradition, one feels empowered to ignore everything that appears philosophical.

Yet, Ancient Greek thought invents the dimension where all the great events forming what we call 'Europe' gradually unfold. To disregard this space would be as if the inhabitants of a city were to disregard the atmosphere surrounding the city. The air that envelops a city is less visible than everything that is done within the city; yet everything is done, and done in the way it is done, only because the air, that particular air, envelops the city. Now, what if this air were fatally polluted?

Generally, one acknowledges that in the European civilization there is a capacity to *produce* and to *destroy* that has no parallel in human history. Europe has transformed the world more than any other civilization has. Nowadays, this capacity to transform has been inherited and tremendously enhanced by the USA–USSR Duumvirate. But it is still an essentially European phenomenon: it is the power over the world emerging from the application of science to industry.

Nonetheless, it is not in a merely quantitative sense that the European civilization is more powerful than the other civilizations. Indeed, there is an undeniable connection between power and scientific rationality. Power depends on one's ability to predict. Yet scientific prediction is preceded by philosophical prediction. The *epistéme* – that is, philosophy in its originary ['originario', t/n] dimension – is the vision of the ultimate Meaning of the world, and therefore, it is the foresight of the essence of all future events. But in order to grasp the authentic meaning of foreseeing, one must bring to light what is seen in the vision. What do the Ancient Greeks see, then? In production and destruction, they begin to see something never seen before.

The more the product is *new*, compared to what already existed, the more intense, radical and vast the production is. In turn, the *greater* the distance the destruction carries us from what continues to exist, the more destructive the destruction is. For the first time in human history, Ancient Greek thought thinks of this novelty and of this distance *in an extreme fashion*. 'In an extreme fashion' means after the emergence of Ancient Greek thought, it is no longer possible to conceive of a meaning of novelty and of distance, according to which the novelty is even more innovative and distance even more distancing. What, though, is this extreme dimension that Ancient Greek thought assigns to the new, which is produced, and to the distance to which destruction leads?

The Ancient Greeks think: what is genuinely and radically new is that which does not yet exist; the new is what used to be *nothing* and thus emerges from its own nothingness. Furthermore, the extreme distance from existence, to which destruction can lead, is not anything already existing, it is not in any sense existing but, once again, it is *nothingness*. The Ancient Greeks are the first to conceive of the absolutely negative meaning of nothingness. Precisely because of this, it is only with the Ancient Greeks that production and destruction begin to be conceived of as the actions ['l'agire', t/n] that make things come out of nothingness and make them return to nothingness, that is as the actions that produce extreme novelty and extreme distance from existence. For the first time, before the eyes of the Ancient Greeks, the extreme form of production and destruction appears and therefore, for the first time humans act with the intention of making things come out of nothingness and of making them return to it. Such a dimension, unveiled by the Ancient Greeks, is the dimension within which all the great events of European history gradually unfold, namely, the great forms of European productivity and destructiveness: from the classical Christian world to the modern economic production, from modern science and from the bourgeois and communist revolutions to the civilization of technics and to the possibility for technics to produce the annihilation of humankind.

Each of these great forms conceives of and realizes itself as a determinate way of creating or destroying a world, that is a determinate way of making a world come out of nothingness or of pushing a world back into nothingness. Thus, undoubtedly, modern science and technics represent a break with the European tradition, yet they are at the same time, the most rigorous and faithful consequences of the Ancient Greek meaning of production and destruction.

But at the foundation of the European will to produce and destroy lies the *faith* ['fede', t/n] that the world is historical, temporal, becoming ['diveniente', t/n]. That is, the faith that the reality in which we find ourselves is already by itself a constant coming from nothingness and returning to nothingness. For example, it is possible to will to dominate the world by controlling the forces that produce and destroy it only if one firstly wants what-is-to-be-dominated ['il dominabile', t/n] to exist, that is has faith that it is so. It is possible to want the transformation of the world only if one firstly believes that it wants the state in which the world lies to be flexible, dissoluble, transformable. Only on the grounds of this *faith* could all the projects of domination that form European history arise. This is the dominant faith of the European consciousness and praxis – and by now, the dominant faith of the entire planet. The faith in the existence of becoming and of what-is-to-be-dominated is the originary form of the will to power. And it is on the grounds of this Ancient Greek faith that, for the first time, the 'human being', as understood by the West, emerges, that is as the principle of action *par excellence*, which is to say of producing and destroying.

The European *tradition* is the will to impose a *limit* on becoming and on the production and destruction of existence. The limit is represented by the immutable and eternal forms and structures that, each time in their turn, have made the interpretation and the toleration of world's becoming possible. In the European tradition, it is through the affirmation of these structures and forms that the faith in the existence of becoming attempts to defend itself from the threat of becoming that it has itself evoked. On the contrary, in an ever more radical manner, Modern Europe realizes that all limits imposed on becoming, all immutable structures and forms, end up making the becoming of reality unthinkable – they end up making unthinkable the very dimension that urges the evocation of the immutable.

In order to be capable of power, the will to power becomes faith in the existence of becoming and of what-is-to-be-dominated; nevertheless, the immutables, with which the will to power defends itself from the threat of becoming that it has itself evoked, make becoming illusory. It transpires that for the modern European human, the terror caused by the domination of the immutable over becoming becomes more unbearable than the terror caused by becoming itself, and that after the attempt of philosophy (and of Christianity), it is science that now offers itself as the true remedy against the threat of becoming. The scientific–technological Apparatus, which by now dominates the planet far beyond the reach of modern Europe, has the capacity to solve the issues regarding its own reproduction and unlimited expansion. In the following pages, this capacity of the Apparatus is brought to light on multiple occasions. Besides, this capacity remains unaffected by the 'humanistic' criticisms continuously directed at the civilization of technics. Indeed, humanism too is a form, by now a dwindling form, of the will to power. Any criticism directed at science and technics, in all the various fields of Western culture, is baseless because it fails to realize the root of the will to power and is itself grounded in this root.

Even if traditional Europe still contends with the modern Europe of science and technics for the right to embody the authentic legacy of Europe in the world, this is a contention that develops entirely within the dominant faith of the European civilization.

As a matter of fact, the legacy of Europe in the world can be traced following two vastly different directions.

On one hand, one can push domination over the Earth ever further (that is, one can push ever further the Ancient Greek dimension of producing and destroying). On this path, technics can get rid of God and of the human being as powerless and restraining forms of domination; yet compromises and convergences between technics, God and humans may still be sought for a long time. After all, compared to technics, God and humans certainly appear as impotent forms of the will to power, but they are nevertheless forms of it: modes by which, in the European tradition, the domination of the world has been devised. On this course, technics can lead to the annihilation of the Earth; but it can also devise tools capable of preventing it. Indeed, on the basis of the faith in the Ancient Greek meaning of becoming and of production and destruction, one can even produce peace and destroy war.

On the other hand, one can grasp the legacy of Europe in a completely different way, along a path never travelled, which has nothing to do with the trends that currently dominate the world. Finally, it is a matter of questioning the essence of Europe – which by now is the essence of the entire planet. It is a matter of questioning what has never been questioned: the fundamental faith of the West, the faith that the world is time, history, becoming, that is the faith that the world is an emerging from nothingness and a returning to it – a faith which is the very originary form of the will to power. It is a matter of pushing the European critical sense to its furthest possibilities: those where thinking ['il pensiero', t/n], instead of continuing to think and to guide actions, shifts to a point *outside* of that faith, while remaining within it in order to look it in the face and measure its significance and weight. In our time, critical sense believes to have nothing left to learn. On the contrary, though its refinement and perfection develops continuously, critical sense remains within the most undisputed, unconscious and untouchable of all dogmas.

Until one questions and makes visible the dominant faith that has enveloped and led the entire course of European civilization, and that by now envelops and leads the entire course of the world, the world wanders in the dark. The lights that light up in it do not dispel the darkness. In their deepest meaning, 'peace', 'salvation', the 'dignity of humans', 'goodwill', and 'reason', which have been contrived to improve the human condition, are dark lights.

If one could look in the face the originary faith of the West, the possibility to grasp the authentic meaning of Europe's productive–destructive essence would present itself for the first time. The will for salvation, which desires peace and remedies for human ills, could itself reveal its authentic face beneath the meanings that are commonly ascribed to it. On this understanding, the authentic legacy of Europe does not consist in the perpetuation of the essence of European reality, but in the thinking in which such an essence finally appears as faith and as the originary form of the will to power.

That is the common theme of the following pages, although they were composed on different occasions. Be that as it may, these pages are such as to intimate an overview, rather than the in-depth analysis which is present in other writings of mine.

1

About the 'crisis'

1

Sixteen years after its publication (1972) and despite the resistance it has met, *The Limits to Growth*, the study entrusted by the Club of Rome to D. H. Meadows and other researchers on the 'dilemmas of humanity', is still deemed an inescapable reference point for the discussion of the meaning of the current 'crisis'. It is the first computer model of long-term global trends (over a century), regarding population, food production, pollution and resource consumption. Its well-known thesis is that if the current trend of economic development stays unchanged, the global economic system will collapse within a few decades due to population growth not matched by adequate food availability, due to the consumption of non-renewable resources, and due to pollution exceeding the limits required for sustaining life on the planet.

The significance of *The Limits to Growth* resides in drawing attention to the issues of the entire planet, taking a viewpoint intending to use the methods and tools of science in depth (a viewpoint that, therefore, has shown willingness to correct the error discovered in the computer program, on which the main projections of the research depended – the only consequence, nonetheless, being that in the modified model the final economic collapse still proves to be not avoidable yet merely delayed, compared to the predictions of the original model).

The main criticism raised against *The Limits to Growth* is that this study combines excessive pessimism concerning human technological capabilities with excessive optimism regarding humanity's willingness to undergo the therapy which the study suggests after its diagnosis. From the equation: capital investment = pollution increase = resource depletion; and from the thesis that capital tends to grow exponentially, *The Limits to Growth* infers that the therapy to be undergone firstly involves reducing capital investment growth to zero. The other side of the therapy involves reducing population growth to zero. After that reduction, the quantity of goods produced and consumed at a zero-level economic growth should be evenly distributed across all global regions, while developed countries should lower their economic level in order to bring the economies of less developed countries to an average level. The optimism of Meadows and his colleagues lies precisely in believing this enormous wealth transfer to be feasible. Their pessimism, on the other hand, lies in not taking into account in any way alternative technologies that may prevent such massive impoverishment and such resource depletion.

In any case, the common approach of *The Limits to Growth* and of its critics is represented by the shared intention to arrange technological capabilities so as to ensure the survival of humankind for as long as it is possible. In this case, the survival instinct is organized on a planetary scale. This instinct – they say – is a fact; science incorporates it, that is, science makes this fact rational by removing any element of individual selfishness from it. The will for humanity to survive – humanity, not just certain human groups – is a force that is slowly and arduously making its way. Furthermore, such a will is becoming a mass force precisely at a time in which the culture of our epoch is realizing that it cannot grant this will any other value than the one given by the extent of its effectiveness. If one believes that the supreme form of knowledge is science, science can indeed provide the most adequate means to ensure the survival of humankind; yet science is not capable of ensuring that such survival *should* be pursued. Max Weber knew this very well. In other words, the will for humanity to survive is a *faith*, which clashes with other faiths. Not only does it clash with faiths that want the survival of a certain human group at the expense of others: it also clashes with a faith like the Christian one, according to which the supreme value and problem of humans is not their survival on Earth but the salvation of their soul.

In a situation where the faith in the impossibility of all definitive truths prevails, what makes or breaks the clash between different faiths (which the dominant faith is aware of) is not their incontrovertible truth – given that they are faiths, precisely because they are not incontrovertible truths – but their practical strength: that is, on one side, their persuasive power, and on the other, the ability of these faiths to persuade that what they suggest ensures the domination over the other faiths and over the world. If, as occurs in our civilization, science is believed to be the only genuine form of knowledge, the strongest faith is the one in whose greater strength one has faith. And precisely, the scientific–technological arrangement of existence is the faith in whose greatest strength one has nowadays faith, and that therefore dominates every other faith and leads it to decline. On the other hand, the faith in the impossibility of all incontrovertible truths substantially coincides with the faith that science be authentic knowledge and that the scientific–technological arrangement is the dominant power.

This domination is also evident in the formulation of the 'fundamental problem of humanity': when one affirms that this problem is the incompatibility between the survival of the human race and the unchecked increase in population and pollution, which result in progressive scarcity of food and resources, not that one neglects the 'problems of the spirit', but one affirms their subordinate nature. The fundamental problem of humanity is what appears as such in the eyes of the faith that dominates over every other faith.

This is not to say that the scientific–technological arrangement should halt at its initial and naiver phase, where so-called 'spiritual values' seem to have no place. On the contrary, the civilization of technics is already far beyond its initial phase and exhibits the capacity to incorporate and enhance even 'spiritual values': simply, it prevents them from insisting upon replacing science and technics in guiding and arranging existence.

2

Yet, the civilization of technics is no solid block. This gathers around two antagonistic poles: the United States and the Soviet Union. For each of these two poles, the fundamental issue is not the survival of humanity but its own survival. After all, it is reasonable to assume that most human groups see their own survival as the supreme value. Nevertheless, when these human groups coincide with the two major existing centres of power on Earth, their will to survive prevails over any similar will.

It is in relation to this unprecedented historical situation that the optimism of the therapy suggested by *The Limits to Growth* becomes extortionate, just as its utopian character. But it must also be immediately noted that this optimism is found even in alternative therapies – as happens, for instance, in books like *The World Challenge* by Servan-Schreiber. Instead of suggesting a zero growth in the world economy in order to achieve an average level of investments and consumption significantly lower than the current level of developed countries and significantly higher than the one of underdeveloped countries, these alternative therapies suggest providing underdeveloped countries with the most sophisticated technologies nowadays available to wealthy nations, so as to elevate the poor to the level of the rich without slowing down the economic growth of the latter.

In both these therapies, one tends to overlook a fact (but it is an extremely widespread tendency), which is just as much elementary as it is crucial. Undoubtedly, the USA and the USSR are in a position to destroy each other, but each of them has become invincible when compared to all other peoples on Earth. And in an increasingly hungry and resource-poor world, those who have become invincible have no intention to relinquish their invincibility or their wealth. This is an essential condition of such an invincibility and is, in turn, ensured by it. It is very hard for social sciences to relinquish this statement given that it is one of their most confirmed hypotheses. Levelling all the economies of the planet – both in the sense suggested by Meadows and in Servan-Schreiber's sense – means abolishing the abyss that the two superpowers (the USA and the USSR) have created between themselves and the others. It means rendering them even more vulnerable than all those peoples who have had to suffocate their will to exist so far.

It is often observed that the mistake of *The Limits to Growth* does not lie in the calculation of the consequences resulting from the current trends of the bio-economic system, but rather in the rigid equation between capital investment, pollution and irreversible resource consumption. In other words, there is general agreement that if current trends perpetuated, the global economic collapse would become unavoidable. Nonetheless, this discourse completely overlooks the variable given by the presence of the two superpowers on the world stage. When realizing the approaching of the point of collapse, these superpowers – even assuming that they would be so lacking in political foresight as to allow the point of collapse to arrive without intervening – would have the means to shift its negative consequences onto weaker and poorer populations.

Even more can be said. In a scenario where hungry masses from all over the world menacingly pushed at the borders of the two empires and were about to breach these borders, one would be able to see that the most credible use of nuclear weapons would not be when the two superpowers targeted each other, but when the victims of controlled holocaust were the starving masses of the world. Such an outcome concerns the entire nuclear relationship between the USA and the USSR. One would have to attribute excessively reduced political capabilities to them, if one were to believe that before directly destroying each other, they would not consider destroying each other through a third party, that is by destroying the third party.

Neither does one take into account that if one of the two superpowers deluded itself into surviving a full-scale atomic clash with its direct adversary, it would then find itself in a position of absolute inferiority compared to the vast masses of China, India, South America and Africa. After all, these would have stayed on the sidelines or would have not been directly affected by the nuclear destruction. This is a further element to rule out the possibility of the most credible use of nuclear armament by the two superpowers be that of a head-on collision scenario.

3

The tension between the two superpowers for world domination creates an extremely dynamic economic conjuncture. Or rather, the most dynamic conjuncture ever seen on Earth.

Without this planet-wide conflict, the prediction belonging to the central part of the scenario suggested by J. A. Schumpeter would very plausibly come true: the prediction regards the increasing mechanization of industrial development and therefore the conclusion of all proper technological innovation, that is, the transformation of innovation itself into routine. For Schumpeter, such a scenario entails the disappearance of the capitalist entrepreneur and thus the decline of capitalism itself. The American New Right and the American school of the 'supply-side economics' embrace Schumpeter's concept, but they do so to proclaim that technological innovation and entrepreneurial spirit are far from dead, and that planning mechanization (hence anti-innovating mechanization) is a specific feature of real socialism, which is therefore destined to lose the game it is playing against capitalism.

Yet, in both cases (and regarding Schumpeter, the reason is a chronological one), the fundamental factor which drives technological innovation with unprecedented intensity on our planet nowadays is not taken into account. As a matter of fact, this is represented by the conflict between the two superpowers and by their determination not to shorten the distance they have been able to establish from other peoples on Earth. This distance makes them invincible. Now, this circumstance produces the highest form of economic dynamism. Indeed, on one hand, the economic-political spheres revolving around the two antagonistic poles (and, albeit to varying degrees, China, India, and all other non-aligned countries) constantly increase their competitiveness and have long been in pursuit of the two superpowers. These, on their part, demand more and more sophisticated technologies to maintain their safe distance from their pursuers. On the other hand, it is precisely the conflict between the USA and the USSR which further drives technological innovation, primarily marked by the continuous modernization of their military apparatuses.

Thus, the two superpowers have become the two planetary entrepreneurs who ensure technological innovation and economic growth. Not only does the entrepreneurial drive shift from individuals to large 'trusts', but from these to the two poles, which 'ultimately' determine every aspect of life on the planet. To this new planetary entrepreneurship, an indefinite future unfolds (where, as in all enterprise, the very possibility of the entrepreneur's extinction – even imminent extinction – is contained). Although in a way unforeseen by Keynes, the State (or better, the Superstate) has become the fundamental animator of economic life.

This means that the 'continuous revolution' of the techniques of capitalist production, brought to light by Marx and embraced by Schumpeter in his definition of capitalism as 'creative destruction' (i.e. the creation of new production, distribution and organization techniques, which inevitably destroy the old ones), continues and perpetuates itself on an even broader scale, represented by the very opposition between the capitalist world and the socialist one. That is to say that the 'continuous revolution' becomes the common denominator of the two worlds. 'Development' knows no limits.

In effect, it is such a continuous upheaval of the technical presuppositions of production taking place in the two superpowers and, at a decreasing rate, in other industrialized countries, that shapes, at the same time, the conditions for both crisis and economic growth – given that the crisis prevails in those countries where the obsolescence (the 'destruction') of techniques prevails over creativity, while in the opposite case growth prevails.

This solidarity between economic growth and crises presents similarities to the solidarity – observed by the economist David Warsh (who deepened the type of investigation launched by H. Phelps Brown and Sheila V. Hopkins of the London School of Economics) – between inflation increases and crucial phases in European history (more exactly, in British history) over the last nine hundred years. The classic diagram depicting the trend of inflation as a fluctuation that peaks during wars (1866, 1918, 1945) but substantially maintains a consistent average level, only represents a very narrow phase of the inflation curve, which on its part is adequately depicted by a diagram where *plateaux* of a few centuries culminate in an inflationary surge leading to a higher *plateau*. An upward line where surges, lasting about a century, are interspersed with *plateaux* lasting either one or two centuries. If the capitalist economy has constantly lied in the last surge since the post-war period (with fluctuations that are irrelevant when compared to the breadth of the diagram), the other three major surges of inflation coincide with the establishment of the feudal system (which in England is delayed compared to the Continent), of mercantilism, and of the industrial revolution. In turn, these three surges coincide with the most significant phases of economic growth in Western history. The increasing complexity in the division of labour, in techniques, in institutions and in services leads to significant hikes in costs and prices, as happens in the initial stages of a business cycle.

In virtue of these considerations, one can note that the current inflationary period may not be a symptom of senescence but of the system's vitality. And the 'system' is precisely the planetary order produced by the tension between the capitalist world and the socialist one – both transitioning from the ideological arrangement to the technological arrangement of technics. This 'vitality', however, is the extreme violence itself of the system, its capacity to dominate over any alternative force present in our civilization.

4

If by 'crisis' the current culture means something different from the 'destructiveness' related to the 'creativity' of the civilization of technics – and therefore, something different from the phenomena accompanying such 'destructiveness'; in other words, if by 'crisis' one means the inability of civilization of technics to survive, then the opinion that this civilization is in a 'crisis' is something that still awaits proof from that culture. As a matter of fact, the civilization of technics is not in crisis even if its creativity demands, among other destructions, the destruction of poor countries or, in rich countries, the destruction of the poorest and weakest.

Certainly, such a scenario produces moral indignation in ever larger segments of the population in wealthy countries. Yet – aside from the fact that such outrage (as a series of surveys seem to attest) grows proportionally to the standard of living and security in which one finds themselves and would therefore be at an extremely low level if those outraged saw their survival seriously threatened due to, let us say, the economic collapse as predicted by

Meadows – the question remains of the value of the morality underlying that outrage. After all, in a world that believes it has permanently left behind the illusion of obtaining absolute truths, no morality can claim to have an absolute truth.

One cannot even claim that the presence of the evil is evident even though one does not know what true good consists of. One can concede that it is evident that fire causes harm. Nonetheless, in many cases, and precisely from a medical perspective, fire has a therapeutic function. Undoubtedly, one can object that fire is one thing as therapy and another as torture. However, then the question begins regarding the purposes of torture – and the purposes can be those of preventing harm to other people. At that point, one no longer has the 'self-evidence' ['evidenza', t/n] of the presence of evil, but rather a scale with unreliable weights that tries to establish what is more evil. Certainly, one may firmly believe that violence should not be exerted on any human being; but this is in fact a belief, a faith: it is not 'self-evidence'.

This in no way excludes that a determinate moral demand might increase its *weight* in the world and push the civilization of technics in a direction where the destruction caused by technological creativity abstains from any destructive act towards humankind. What I mean to say is that in a situation where one believes one has nothing to do with the dream of an absolute and incontrovertible truth, the influence of a certain moral demand on the civilization of technics cannot be grounded in the truth of that demand, but in the *practical force* which this demand possesses to modify the development of history. Nevertheless, a scenario is still distant – indeed, it is utopian – in which the existence of humans is guided by moral force with the same intensity, imperativeness and breadth with which human existence is currently guided by technoscientific force.

It is not the civilization of technics that is in crisis, but the forms of Western tradition, which are brought to a close by the mentioned civilization. Not only does the creation of new technologies destroy obsolete technologies, for the civilization of technics as a whole destroys the traditional forms in which Western 'technics' has developed over time: religion, morality, politics, art, philosophy. These forms are destroyed not in the sense of being banned, but in the sense that their claim to guide humanity is denied: such denial does not consist in a mere theoretical act but in the greater *power* of scientific–technological rationality compared to all other forms of rationality. The crisis of 'traditional values' is but their impotence in the face of technological power.

All criticisms directed at the civilization of technics by 'our' culture is grounded in the very attitude of which the civilization of technics is the most rigorous development. This attitude – emerging with the very emergence of human beings – is represented by the conviction of being masters of one's actions and capable of mastering, through actions, the entities of the world. The East has particularly cultivated the ability to become masters of one's inner world; the West has particularly cultivated the ability to become masters of one's external world. Even those philosophers who, like Heidegger (in whom some typical forms of Eastern wisdom echo), question the means-end relationship, simply protest against the *way* in which this relationship takes place today, not the relationship in general. Also for Heidegger, the ancient art of making a pitcher is entirely different from a modern hydroelectric plant. Yet, despite all the undeniable differences, the ancient and the new ways of making things have in common the essential and the crucial: the persuasion (the faith) that the human being is capable of dominating the world, that is, of transforming the world in accordance with their own plans.

This persuasion is so 'natural' that one generally does not want to waste time upon it. The essence of this persuasion remains unchanged even when it is noted that the authentic historical actors are not individuals, but groups, apparatuses, institutions, structures. (This is the current version of the traditional concept that the authentic historical actor is the divine.) Such a persuasion is so 'natural' precisely because it is the 'nature' itself of humans. The civilization of technics is the full unfolding of the 'nature' of humans.

The supreme question begins here. In its full unfolding, the nature of humans especially wants to talk about 'concrete problems' and solutions that indicate 'what we must do'. On the other hand, the nature of humans gets annoyed if one talks about the possibility that the human being is an error (which is an utterly different assertion from the banal verdict, according to which humans make mistakes). The nature of humans gets even more annoyed if one says that the affirmation 'the human being is an error' has an entirely different meaning from the one it has in some sectors of 'our' culture. According to Nietzsche, for example, the human being is an error and must transform into an 'Übermensch'. Yet Nietzsche's overman shares the essential features of the civilization of technics. In fact, in Nietzsche's overman, the persuasion of being the master of the world reaches its peak.

On the contrary, when thinking that the human being is an error, it is a matter of recognizing in the 'overman' – that is, in what lies beyond the human – the *twilight* of the persuasion of being the masters of things. If one follows this train of thought, one embarks on the path where the true but deeply hidden meaning of the 'crisis' of the civilization of technics reveals itself – the true meaning of the 'limit' to growth. Along this path, one will have to linger long on what the current culture takes for granted: having permanently left behind the old dream of 'truth'.

2

The fundamental tendency of our time and the meaning of the future

1

The tools available to human beings tend to transform their own nature. From means, they tend to become purposes. Nowadays, this phenomenon has reached its most radical form. The totality of tools in advanced societies is becoming the fundamental purpose of these societies. In the sense that they aim especially at increasing the power of their tools. The ancients already knew that if the purpose of wealth is to live well, it may also happen that one ends up pursuing wealth as the purpose itself of one's life. In this way, wealth, which initially represented a means, a tool, becomes a purpose, an end.

The tool gives its user a certain power, allowing them to achieve determinate purposes. Modern natural science has enabled a dizzying increase in the power of tools. Thus emerged the tools of modern technology. Nonetheless, their power is not exclusively due to physics and mathematics: it is also due to the configuration of the society that employs scientific technology. Without a sufficiently developed legal, economic, political, bureaucratic, educational, financial, urban and health system, the most powerful tools of physical–mathematical technology could not function for a single moment. Besides, in industrially advanced societies, the type of rules structuring the economy, bureaucracy, law, the education system, etc., is more and more similar to the rules of the formation of scientific knowledge and its application to industry. Thus, science and scientific technology integrate into the set of systems that make possible the effectiveness of tools which are brought to light by the scientific–technological system. This integration forms a single large Apparatus. This is the supreme tool: the organization of all the tools available to advanced societies, the supreme power at the human disposal.

But such an Apparatus is not evenly distributed on Earth. The Apparatus is the fundamental feature of the rich world, both the capitalist and the communist, and especially of the two centres of these worlds: the United States and the Soviet Union.

Real socialism and capitalism have the power to modify the fate of the world because, in both of them, scientific–technological rationality prevails or is prevailing over those forms of civilization and culture, which make the two systems distinguished and opposed. In other words, the immense variety of events in the world is now gathered into a unity and led into a unified direction not by the great traditional forms of Western civilization, which share, by the way, this vocation (Christianity, capitalism, Marxist socialism), but by the dominance that the two systems have over the world thanks to their scientific–technological Apparatus.

In its essence, the Apparatus is a planning structure (*ad-paratus, ad-parare*); that is, it is a capacity – or rather, the highest capacity ever to appear in human history – to arrange means that are suitable for achieving purposes. Certainly, real socialism and capitalism (as well as Christianity and liberal democracy) intend to tailor the Apparatus to their own purposes; even science still declares that it can only be 'neutral' with regards to purposes, that is, it cannot, as science, suggest purposes. However, the effectiveness of the Apparatus is not given by the determinate purpose to which the Apparatus is dedicated (that is, by the fact that within the Apparatus one pursues this rather than that purpose to which the Apparatus has been set from the outside): when the Apparatus manages to free itself from the will to arrange the means according to criteria of an 'ideological' kind – i.e. different from those indicated by scientific rationality – its effectiveness no longer depends on the kind of purpose to which the Apparatus is set (even though under equal conditions, that is, under equal effectiveness, certain goals are obviously more accessible than others). This is to say that whatever the external purpose assigned to the Apparatus may be, this possesses *in itself* a supreme purpose: *that of reproducing itself and of indefinitely increasing its capacity to achieve purposes.*

Yet all 'ideologies' – this term is nowadays meant as any human attitude that differs more or less profoundly from scientific–technological rationality and from the level currently achieved by it – are concerned with realizing such a supreme purpose of the Apparatus. Therefore, this purpose establishes itself as the purpose of every ideology and thus ceases to be its mere instrument. Precisely for this reason, the supreme end of the scientific–technological Apparatus becomes the measure of every ideological end: in the sense that the latter must not prevent the growth of the Apparatus' power – given that, preventing the growth of the Apparatus, the ideological end itself would reduce the degree of its own realizability. Yet, not constituting an obstacle is already a form of subordination to what must not be prevented, particularly when one observes that one's antagonistic ideology allows greater freedom for the development of the Apparatus.

Nevertheless, in the United States and the Soviet Union – the centres of the two systems of forces from whose resultant the course of the world currently originates – the most eye-catching aspect of the growth of the power of the Apparatus is given by the growth of its destructive power. For this reason, too, 'ideologies' still believe they have the right to measure, judge, and possibly condemn the will of the Apparatus to indefinitely increase its power.

Furthermore, inevitably, the structure that plans the indefinite increase of its power is also the will to prevent its own destruction.

Certainly, the current technological level of this planning structure nowadays allows the two antagonistic systems, in which it is realized, to prevent their own destruction only by preparing the nuclear destruction of the opponent. The two antagonistic planetary systems clash as 'ideologies'; but each of the two is inhabited by the same Apparatus of scientific rationality. In this scenario, the infinite will to power, which is inevitably a will to perpetuate itself and therefore not to be destroyed, certainly actualizes as a contradiction, for the way in which power defends the perpetuation of its growth, if the defence were effectively put into action, would produce the destruction of power itself. Thus, the ideological clash binds the will to power to the total destructiveness of atomic conflict.

On the other hand, this is in fact a contradiction not concerning the scientifically rational will to indefinitely increase the will's own power: It concerns the ideological ground in which such a will finds itself growing. Moreover, only this contradictory situation nowadays enables the defence and hence the (undoubtedly precarious) survival of the supreme form of the will to power. Additionally, if today the ideological clash ensures that this form prevents its own destruction only by preparing the destruction of the antagonistic ideological system, and therefore only by preparing its own destruction, this is not the only conceivable way in which the scientific–technological Apparatus can prevent its annihilation. In addition to the possibility of non-destructive defence techniques, the possibility remains that the planetary ideological clash will subside, especially once it is accepted that technics can achieve the fundamental aims that ideologies aim for – primarily the liberation of humanity from pain.

Yet in the meantime, even though ideologies are interested in the indefinite growth of the power available to human beings, they cannot accept the

Apparatus (in which such a growth takes shape) being defenceless against the threat of destruction. 'Ideologies' – including the most peaceful and edifying ones – do not criticize the infinite self-assertion of the will to power: they criticize the antagonistic 'ideology' that has been able to administer that self-affirmation. Therefore, ideologies contend for the management of power. Thus, the pure will to indefinitely more power remains the purpose to which every ideology has an interest in subordinating its own ends.

2

Even the belief that it is the human being who should control technics and not technics controlling the human being has an ideological character. The opposition between the 'inhumanity' of technics and the 'humanity' of human beings fails to consider that the 'human being', in its deepest essence, is technics, that is will to power; and that technics and science become 'inhuman' when they are arbitrarily identified with their most naively reductive features. The essence of art and of every religion is technical; just as the essence of love or philosophy is technical. At any rate, the aim is to dominate the world (external or internal, of this side or of the other). After all, even the opposition between 'ideology' and scientific–technological rationality is the opposition between different forms of technics, that is, different forms of the will to power. The 'ideologies' are the forms of the will to power that lose out to the winning form, which we are here referring to as the 'scientific–technological Apparatus'. Even all forms of humanism are ever more compelled to subordinate their purposes to the supreme goal of the Apparatus; however, it is within the scientific–technological Apparatus that the essence of the human – the technical essence of the human – presents its most faithful and profound expression – an essence which stays disguised in every form of humanism.

Nevertheless, all this has nothing to do with an apology of the civilization of technics and of the will to power. It is true that our culture, in its essence, cannot criticize scientific rationality and the kind of civilization corresponding to it. But 'our' culture *is not all* (and the term 'culture' also refers, here, to the non-Western forms of our culture). With regards to scientific rationality and the civilization produced by it, one can repeat what Freud used to say about religion: *It is the most radical alienation* that allows those who are alienated to free themselves from all shallower and less severe forms of alienation. In other words, scientific–technological rationality is the most rigorous rationalization of the negativity of alienation. Except that even psychoanalysis is a form of scientific rationality. And above all, the true meaning of 'alienation' remains essentially inaccessible to every 'culture', that is, to every cultivation of the will to power. Besides, indicating the true essence of alienation does not mean suggesting a therapy, for every therapy and every will for salvation belong to the essence itself of alienation. Yet, one of the greatest cultural miseries of our time is the casualness of the belief that 'alienation' can be identified with the will to power. Faced with this attitude, the will to power has every right to retort that such identification only expresses the envy of the losers. The criticisms directed by our time at the will to power only serve to mask the abyss that opens within it.

3

There is another reason why the purposes of 'ideology' must allow themselves to be measured and judged by the prevailing form of the will to power. Indeed, contemporary culture (from science to philosophy) believes that the attempt to possess an incontrovertible and unmodifiable truth – the great adventure of philosophy – has failed. Thus, no purpose can assume that the law demanding its realization is an incontrovertible and unmodifiable truth. Therefore, in this circumstance, the value of a purpose is *solely* represented by its capacity to be realized, subordinating or preventing the realization of its alternative purposes; and any knowledge aiming to justify the choice of a purpose is but a *faith* – that is, inasmuch as it intends to persuade, it is a form of 'rhetoric' (precisely in the Aristotelian sense of the term).

But precisely because the scientific–technological will to infinitely increase the will's power is capable of subordinating the realization of any other purpose to its own realization, this will becomes the supreme value or, if one still cares about using this word, this will becomes the supreme 'truth' (i.e. the supreme 'rhetoric') of our time. This means that it has the 'right' to measure and judge every other purpose.

Hence, it is inevitable that all faiths perceive, even implicitly, their own nature as nothing but faith, as well as they perceive their impotence when comparing themselves to the faith of which science itself consists. And such a perception, even when unexpressed, already represents the subordination of 'ideological' faiths to scientific faith: It represents their deep-seated renunciation of dominance over the world – even though they continue to proclaim the right to this dominance with their lips. Christian faith, for instance, asserts that true power does not appear in this world. But either this faith concedes that it is losing in the world (or that it is at least subordinate), or it plans to conquer the hearts of humans: but then the heart is guided by Christian love, which thus becomes the supreme power *in* the world, that is the rigorous configuration of the will to infinitely increase the will's own power (since even love knows no bounds to its edification).

But there is no sign that Christian love (or any other form of the will to power) is about to replace scientific rationality in ruling the world. Rather, the opposite is occurring: In the capitalist system and in the socialist one, the 'ideological' organization of existence is increasingly giving way to its scientific–technological organization. (And thus, the ideological organization of technics is increasingly giving way to the technical arrangement of technics.) *This is the fundamental 'tendency' currently underway on Earth.* In effect, all analyses aiming to enlighten the trends developing in the capitalist and socialist subsystems must refer to it. In other words, there is an ongoing process in which the Apparatus of scientific–technological rationality not only diminishes the resistance that ideologies put up to it within the two systems but also questions the very existence of such systems, an existence depending on their ideological opposition.

4

All this means that each of the two systems is a *contradiction*, i.e. a form of the 'objective spirit' (to use a Hegelian expression), in which the principle of non-contradiction is negated. This is a contradiction between the goal of the Apparatus and the goal of ideologies. In that sense, even the supersystem formed by the relationship between the two systems is a contradiction in that it forms a unity, despite the antagonism of its terms. Now, it is precisely due to this contradiction between ideologies and scientific rationality that the scientific will to defend the will's own indefinite growth takes place today as the contradiction discussed earlier, which consists in defending itself by arranging the will's own destruction.

Every clash between purposes is a 'contradiction' in that the relationship, the unity formed by the relationship between antagonistic purposes, represents a sort of code which contains mutually contradictory prescriptions. Said otherwise, this code is a *self-contradiction* ['contraddirsi', t/n]. Therefore, the code is not simply the 'real opposition' between forces, which according to Kant is 'without (logical) contradiction'; but it is a 'real opposition' that is *at once* a logical contradiction. (Not in the sense, however, that what is negated by the principle of non-contradiction is real, but in the sense that the *self-contradiction* that forms the clash between purposes is real.)

Thus, the fundamental tendency of our time is the progressive prevalence of scientific rationality within the contradiction between such rationality and ideologies. At the same time, this tendency is the perpetuation of a substantial balance in the other contradiction mentioned: the one where, in the global supersystem, the capitalist and socialist systems are opposing each other.

Therefore, in the present context, the term 'tendency' does not simply allude to the observable frequency of a certain phenomenon (which may potentially become the basis for a probabilistic prediction): indeed, from a mere statistical-probabilistic perspective, where the tendency is essentially a frequency, not only is every tendency reversible, but every regression of the tendency has the same legitimacy as its corresponding progression. From a mere scientific perspective, one cannot rule out the possibility of ideology 'legitimately' taking the reins of the world again. And even if science still disregards the relationship between contradiction and tendency, the fundamental tendency of our civilization is the progressive domination of one of the two terms forming the contradiction between ideology and the scientific–technological Apparatus.

Therefore, the contradiction is the very state of instability which, though being a necessary condition, is not a sufficient condition for the establishment of a tendency. Indeed, contradiction as such does not incontrovertibly show in which direction it will be solved ['tolta', t/n], i.e. it does not reveal which of its two constituent elements prevails. This prevalence is an *occurrence*, a fact that cannot be incontrovertibly predicted by analysing the content of the contradiction. (In other words, the forecast here is a mere conjecture.) On the contrary, Hegel and Marx mistakenly identify the necessary condition with the sufficient condition of the tendency and of the actual becoming ['divenire effettivo', t/n]: Therefore, they are led to affirm that the occurrence of the contradiction necessarily implies the occurrence of a state of the world in which the contradiction is solved.

In this context, it is particularly relevant to note that the contradiction between scientific rationality and ideology does not – yet – mean that ideology itself is a contradiction.[1] The second part of this chapter will attempt to bring to light the *essential* contradiction within which the entire Western tradition, and hence every ideology, operates: an essential contradiction that is still completely missed by scientific–technological rationality, which for its part represents the overcoming of the contradiction discussed above.

In the meantime, it should also be noted that identifying the fundamental 'tendency' of our time does not require any prediction: This is simply a process that has been ongoing for some time and continues to evolve; one can consider it an 'observable phenomenon', provided that certain rules of interpretation of what is effectively observable are adopted: those rules, which are in the present context *presumed* to guide the interpretation organizing the current human experience of the world (where this 'presumption' is itself an effect of the application of those rules of interpretation). Such tendency would be there even if the most abrupt of reversals were imminent and were about to invert it. As mentioned, however, the contradiction that produces the instability of this tendency does not in any way suggest the direction of its future development.

5

On the other hand, the research developed in *The Limits to Growth* (see Chapter 1) appears to be a prediction that has recently received substantial confirmation at the international conference of the Club of Rome held in Budapest. According to the 'Report' of this research, predicting the collapse of the civilization of technics ['civiltà della tecnica', t/n] does not necessarily require taking into account the growth of the atomic armaments of the two superpowers. Properly speaking, however, this is no prediction, but a tautology, i.e. an analytical statement. Indeed, it is the affirmation that, given certain variables (resources, population, pollution), and assuming their regular variation, it is possible to mathematically predict their specific relationship after a certain period. On the other hand, authentic scientific prediction is a *hypothetical* (probabilistic) anticipation of the future based on past experiences. Besides, the hypothetical and probabilistic nature of a prediction excludes it from being a tautology. As is known, the 'Report' commissioned by the Club of Rome took into account certain variables while refusing to consider other variables, such as alternative technologies and unforeseen technologies. But above all, and as previously mentioned, the 'Report' has not considered the fact that the two superpowers, having become invincible compared to the rest of the world, have no intention whatsoever of relinquishing this extraordinary privilege, which is unprecedented in human history. In other words, it is predictable (this time, according to the meaning that science attributes to 'predictability') that long before the occurrence of the global collapse predicted by the 'Report', the two superpowers (and to a lesser extent, the systems they are the centres of) will dissociate their destinies from those of a starving humanity. Nowadays, the possibility of an atomic clash between the USA and USSR is deemed 'realistic'. Nonetheless, this 'realism' is naive if compared to the prediction that the privileged peoples of the Earth will not use their power to destroy each other but rather to survive in an increasingly uninhabitable world. (Hence the danger for the subsystems of the two planetary systems to move away from the centre of their respective systems.) If the scientific–technological Apparatus, nowadays represented by the privileged countries, consists in a will to indefinitely increase the will's own power – therefore, if the scientific–technological Apparatus consists in a will to prevent the will's own destruction, the possibility of its collapse due to scarcity of resources in relation to the world population is extremely unlikely compared to the possibility that the Apparatus will destroy those attempting to deprive it of the resources it needs to survive and grow. Along this path, where rich countries destroy the poorer ones, the contradiction mentioned earlier, which is represented by the possibility that the wealthy destroy each other (that is, the possibility that the Apparatus is forced to destroy itself to protect itself), also vanishes. Additionally, it is highly improbable that the centres of planetary rationality would decide to halt the fundamental tendency of their development and that they would prefer, through more or less direct force, to eliminate the human masses deemed surplus compared to the available resources (on the basis of the perpetuation of the current functioning of the Apparatus), instead of removing ideological obstacles that prevent the optimal functioning of the Apparatus. From this perspective, the constant advancement of military technologies ensures the continuation of the process through which scientific–technological rationality liberates itself from ideological obstacles.[2]

6

The fundamental tendency ongoing on Earth is the shift from the ideological to the technological arrangement of existence, in the sense that the progressive removal of the ideological barriers to scientific rationality is an observable phenomenon, by now widely acknowledged (always provided that one assumes – once again – the rules governing the interpretation of empirical data that are in this book presume to govern the current human experience of the world). Both in the capitalist and socialist worlds, the rationalization of economic production is leading to the abandonment of the ideological management of the economy. The Soviet Union pioneered an entire sector of economic science – the theory of economic planning – which was entirely absent in Marx's writings. In an analogous way, the capitalist world has constantly revolutionized its mode of production, introducing increasingly efficient technologies that have caused Western masses to abandon their traditional behaviours and beliefs more quickly than in socialist countries. The dysfunction and inadequacy of institutions exist in relation to the scientific–technological *mode of production*. Obsolete institutions express ideologies, i.e. outdated forms of the will to power. The conflict between declining and crystallized forms versus the victorious and fluid form of the will to power – that is, the conflict between ideologies and scientific–technological rationality – is once again, and at its maximum extent, the contradiction between social relations and a mode of production that no longer finds itself at ease within them and therefore tends to break free from them. Indeed, the will to power is the will for production – and hence for destruction, because the former is inconceivable without the latter, as Schumpeter meant to express, at an economic level, by defining capitalism as 'creative destruction'.

The fundamental tendency of our civilization is present in Italy as well, albeit encountering greater resistance than in the other industrialized Western countries. In Italy, the delayed development of the economic basis of scientific–technological rationality combines with the presence of two major ideological forces: the world centre of Catholicism (and its political and social projections onto national life) and the strongest communist party in the West. Both the progressive detachment of Italian society from religious codes of conduct, and the fact that the Italian Communist Party (PCI) distances itself from Marxism more and more sharply, are symptoms of the fundamental tendency.

7

But the true meaning of this tendency does not come to light – and even the example of the Italian situation diminishes to a banality – as long as the transition from traditional civilization to the civilization of technics is deemed a mere *fact*. It is not even sufficient to acknowledge that the basis of this 'fact' is given by the contradiction between ideological and scientific–technological purposes of the will to power. Rather, one should delve into the very essence of Western civilization, that is, into the essence of the supreme form of the will to power, overcoming what the West, and therefore modern science itself, knows about itself – and thus overcoming all form of motivation on the basis of which scientific rationality is convinced it has dispensed with ideologies. One should descend into the Ancient Greek soul of our civilization. Only thus can the authentic meaning that *time*, and therefore the *future*, have within the civilization of technics.

The will to power can be the will to dominate and infinitely increase its own dominance only because, first and foremost, it *wants what-is-to-be-dominated to exist*. Undoubtedly, in all forms of civilization (that is, in all forms of the will to power), one believes that the existence of what-is-to-be-dominated (nature, humans, and even gods) is not an object of will, but something given in and of itself and independent of the will. Nonetheless, *to believe, to have faith* in the existence of what-is-to-be-dominated and in its being given to the will, precisely means *to want* what-is-to-be-dominated to exist and to be something given. Faith and will are the same thing. Therefore, the will wants first and foremost the existence of its own playing field.

On one hand, wanting the existence of what-is-to-be-dominated means wanting every bond of things with their 'ground' to be dissoluble; on the other, it means wanting things to be purposes and means of one's will. When trees are cut (to obtain, for example, construction lumber), their bond with the ground is dissolved. Yet one can decide to cut trees only if, on one hand, *one believes* that their bond with their ground is dissoluble (i.e. only if *one wants* this dissolubility to exist), and on the other hand, only if *one believes* (that is, if *one wants*) that there exists a system of means and purposes which is dependent on the will and within which the cutting of trees and construction works fall. Said otherwise, the will does not restrict itself to wanting to dominate the world: *the will wants the world itself to be* (even if, from its own perspective, the will regards the world as something given in and of itself and independent of the will).

The will for the world to be joins the will for the world to be a system of means and purposes, because of the vertigo from which the will is overtaken when it evokes the world. In fact, by wanting what-is-to-be-dominated to exist, the will unleashes the extreme danger before its eyes. Released from every bond with a ground, things burst unpredictably into existence and threaten to upheave its core. The danger and bewilderment of existence rise from the very unpredictability of events.

Therefore, the *prediction* of events is the fundamental way in which existence defends itself from the vertigo of the unpredictable. (And existence is in effect the will to power, which is both the will for survival and for salvation.) Certainly, the will can intervene in the world that the will itself has evoked only if the will believes that the world is a system of means and purposes it can control; and having control of this system means predicting which purposes can be achieved with certain means. But already prediction *as such* – independently of its use in the means–purpose scheme – brings events *under a rule*, and their threat is distanced precisely by the transparency that the events of the world acquire when brought under the rule. Prediction is an even more originary form of the will to power than the one represented by the coordination of means to purposes.

8

With the advent of Western civilization, the will to power realizes its extreme possibilities – although Western culture still struggles to grasp the unprecedented greatness of its own origins, and although modern science still tends to emphasize its detachment from them rather than its deep and substantial solidarity with them. The origin of the West, and the ground in which the West grows and continues to be collocated, is the Ancient Greek meditation on the meaning of *being* and *nothingness* ['dell'essere e del niente', t/n]. Indeed, the will (i.e. the faith) that what-is-be-dominated exists dissolves every bond of things with their *being* and their *nothingness*; the will to power of the West, wanting the existence itself of the world, wants the world to be the coming out of nothingness and the return to it. The West believes (that is, wants) that what-is-to-be-dominated exists, in the sense that it believes (wants) that what-is-to-be-dominated is the bustle, the oscillation of things between being and nothingness. And the West believes (wants) that this oscillation is visible, and in fact the maximally visible. What could be more evident for things – so exclaims Western wisdom – than their coming out of nothingness and their returning to it? In other words, the will to power wants becoming, i.e. the oscillation between being and nothingness, to be visible, and in fact the most visible.

But the emergence of this oscillation is at once the looming of the extreme threat: the unpredictable is now what comes *from nothingness*, and what used to be nothing is the *absolutely* unpredictable. Here, the vertigo of the unpredictable seizes rising from an abyss without a bottom. In this context, the fact that Greek tragedy arises in the context of the Ancient Greek meditation on the meaning of being and nothingness has not yet been given sufficient attention.[3]

9

However, just as it evokes the extreme form *of danger*, so does the will to power of the West also evoke the extreme forms *of defence* against danger, namely the two most powerful forms of prediction: the one around which the knowledge of Western tradition gathers and the one culminating in scientific–technological rationality.

At first, the prevision is *philosophy* itself, that is, the *will for 'truth'*. The 'truth' aims to indicate the definitive and incontrovertible meaning of the Whole: it anticipates the essence of every future; therefore, in the face of 'truth', the unpredictable dissolves. Yet, the dissolving of the unpredictable is at once the dissolving of becoming (that is, the process of coming forth from nothingness); and in philosophical thought, as in the entire Western culture and civilization, the will to power wants becoming to be supremely visible and evident. The will to power wants such visibility even when, as often happens in scientific knowledge, it is reluctant to express it. The *prevision*, in which the will for 'truth' consists, makes becoming impossible. In addition, the *vision* (the self-evidence) of becoming is what the will to power of the West originarily ['originariamente', t/n] wants. In other words, by wanting to defend itself against becoming, the will to power, in the form of a will for 'truth', ends up denying the existence of what it wants to defend itself against and, therefore, recognizes it as existing and as supremely visible.

Indeed, if 'truth' exists, becoming (that is, the coming out from nothingness) cannot exist, because what should come from nothingness could not escape the laws of 'truth', and therefore, what should be still nothing ['un ancor niente', t/n] before its existence is already a being ['un essente', t/n] (a listener of 'truth'); so that when it is born, its novelty is entirely fictitious.[4] The future is thus erased: the will for 'truth' *makes nothingness*, out of which things arise in becoming, *be*. The future is identified with the present. In the Western tradition, the meaning of the future is the vanishing of the future.

This entification ['entificazione', t/n] of nothingness (which renders the future a mere appearance and thus nullifies becoming) is not only caused by the will for an immutable 'truth', but also by the will for this 'truth' to affirm the existence of immutable entities and structures. Alongside the immutable 'truth', the immutables with which Western tradition has tried to defend itself against becoming have been God, the immortal soul of humans, the laws of nature, the laws of society understood as natural laws, the laws of historical development, religious and political faiths, 'common sense'. Indeed, every immutable anticipates and foresees the meaning of everything that will gather around it.

10

The immutables render impossible the becoming they wish to regulate; in addition, becoming (the oscillation between being and into nothingness) is what the West *originarily wants* – because only by wanting the movement into being and nothingness to exist can the will to power aim to exercise definitive domination, which assigns things to being and to nothingness. This is to say that, in the history of the West, the vision of becoming is *destined* to destroy the prevision represented by the will for 'truth', that is, by philosophy (in front of which, incidentally, the vision of becoming first comes to light and around which Western tradition gathers). The will to power, wanting the vision of becoming to exist, is *destined* to destroy those forms of the will to power – namely, the will for 'truth' and all the immutables it has evoked – in which nothingness, from which one wants that things come, is transformed into a being.

Until one becomes aware of this entification of nothingness[5] – which represents the true meaning of the nullification of the future within the will for 'truth', i.e., within Western tradition – until the dominant rationality considers the reflection upon the meaning of being and nothingness as mere archaism, every criticism and rejection of tradition by contemporary civilization can simply express the greater *factual* power of scientific–technological rationality over traditional forms of the will to power. Yet a mere *factual* circumstance can be replaced, in an equally legitimate way, by the opposite factual circumstance (even if one believes that such a transformation is not yet on the horizon).

If the fundamental tendency existing on Earth today is the prevalence of the scientific-technological arrangement over the ideological arrangement of existence, that is, in substance, the prevalence of science over philosophy, the essential meaning of this tendency (still hidden to our culture) is the *destination* of the will of 'truth' (and of all immutables) to disappear into scientific-technological rationality. Because of this *destination*, the fundamental tendency of today's world is not limited to what can be said on it from the standpoint of the social and statistical sciences and, in general, from the standpoint of today's entire culture. 'Destination' means that within the scientific-technological will to power, *the contradiction* that, in the will for 'truth', entifies ['entifica', t/n] nothingness and nullifies the future, *is solved* ['tolta', t/n]. Nowadays, science is unable to negate the will for 'truth'; the negation of 'truth' cannot be 'truth': Such negation can only be violence (but violence is also the highest value that can exist if one believes that 'truth' does not exist). But science is the realm where the will for 'truth' is *destined* to decline. In other words, science has not yet realized to be the most rigorous expression of the meaning of becoming brought to light once and for all by Ancient Greek philosophy (and which philosophical thought, by evoking the immutables, has rendered impossible).

In effect, what was presented at the beginning of this chapter as the subordination of ideological purposes to the peculiar purpose of scientific-technological rationality (namely, the purpose represented by the indefinite increase in power) is, *in its essence*, the process in which such rationality destroys the immutables. By making the future illusory, the immutables illusorily dominate becoming and thus are swamped by the irruption of the unpredictable. Indeed, the purposes of Western tradition are pursued within the conviction that reality has an immutable meaning. By making becoming illusory, the immutable meaning of reality makes actions themselves illusory and therefore ineffective. Therefore, the destruction of the immutables – the liberation from them – liberates becoming and actions. The scientific-technological Apparatus is the realm where this destruction–liberation is brought to its extreme possibilities. Aimed at the infinite growth of its power, the Apparatus rules out, in principle, the existence of anything immutable, i.e. of something that the Apparatus would not be able to bring within its own dominance. Reflecting upon itself, the will for becoming *does not* become aware of its will for the *existence of becoming* (the belief in the existence of becoming does not acknowledge to be a belief) but appears to itself as the will to *make* the world *become*. In the Western tradition, the immutables present themselves as the limits to the will to make the world become (the unchangeable limits); as the will to infinitely increase its own power, the Apparatus is the radical destruction of these limits and therefore stands as the centre and as the very driving force of the world's becoming.

By now, the mass of events and practical–theoretical attitudes through which modern and contemporary civilization liberates itself from every form which, presuming to be immutable, prevents the so-called 'novelty' of becoming, is gigantic. The less one understands the authentic meaning of liberation and innovation that are celebrated within it, the more gigantic this mass is: that is, the less one understands that *the will to destroy the immutables is, in its deepest essence, the will to solve ['togliere', t/n] the contradiction where nothingness, in which the future consists, is transformed into a being*, the more gigantic this mass is.

11

Above all, it is scientific reason – albeit unconsciously – that restores to nothingness, from which things originate, its character of nothingness.[6]

If the defence against the threat of the unpredictability of becoming is given by prevision, and if, in the will for 'truth', prevision entifies nothingness (and thus the defence and the domination fail), the experimental method of modern science does not impose its predictions on the becoming of the world (that is, it does not understand prevision as an immutable truth), but lets becoming itself establish the value of prediction; said otherwise, the experimental method grasps prediction as a *test*, a *hypothesis* that, even when it is confirmed in most cases, can always be refuted. Nonetheless, that from which the most confirmed hypothesis can always be refuted can only be that which has no connection with what exists, no predisposition towards what exists, and therefore cannot be anticipated in any way and is absolutely unpredictable; and this can only be that which, emerging in experience, comes *from nothingness*. It is impossible to understand the authentic meaning of the experimental method without considering its relationship with the Ancient Greek meaning of being and nothingness. That is to say that science is not yet in a position to understand what science itself is allowed to understand of its own essence.

Exactly because, according to the essence of scientific rationality, the future is the nothingness from which what exists emerges, the success of any scientific prediction is entirely *casual*: in fact, there cannot be any rule or law driving nothingness to become a being in one direction rather than another. If one retorts that if a rule of occurrence cannot be derived from nothingness, it can nevertheless undoubtedly be derived from what exists, then it is, once again, a matter of establishing whether such a rule is a prediction made by the will for 'truth', which nullifies the future by entifying ['entificando', t/n] nothingness, or whether the rule is a prediction offered by the experimental hypothesis of modern science, which certainly safeguards the nothingness of nothingness ['la nientità del niente', t/n] (i.e. it safeguards the future), but precisely for this reason, is situated in a process where every confirmation of the prediction is entirely casual. This is not to deny the empirical regularities upon which scientific theory and practice organize themselves: it is to say that the Ancient

Greek meaning of becoming, which underlies science, requires the very establishment of any empirical regularity to be an *occurrence*, i.e. an *occurring* onto what exists ['un *caso*, cioè un *cadere* sull'esistente', t/n], emerging from nothing.

Scientific–technological rationality manages to be the most powerful form of prediction and therefore of domination, precisely because, by destroying the will for 'truth' that nullifies the future, such rationality remains open to the absolute unpredictability of the nothingness in which the future consists (i.e. it is entirely willing to modify its theoretical–practical structure, on the basis of the unpredictable that gradually emerges in experience). But this is to say that the power and domination that such rationality manages to exert on the world are absolutely groundless, that is, they are a mere *occurrence* that oc–curs over the course of the world's becoming (and that exactly for this reason, could suddenly cease to occur). The will to endlessly increase one's power takes advantage of this oc–currence of its own power, experimenting all the possibilities of scientific rationality. Therefore, stating that the world's domination achieved by science is chance does not mean stating that science relinquishes coordinating means to purposes on the basis of the most rigorous observation and theoretical elaboration of experience; yet, once again, it means that no matter how significant the mass of empirical regularities confirming the success of the coordination of certain means to certain purposes might be, every purpose which one believes one has achieved is let *oc–cur* onto the world coming from nothingness. It is within such an *oc–currence* that the scientific–technological Apparatus achieves its most extraordinary results.

In other words, it is indisputable that the will to power dominates the world in that this will consists in the scientific–technological Apparatus whose contents and methods are rigorously devised; however, even if the hypotheses by virtue of which the Apparatus plans the domination are constantly confirmed, the fact that the events of the world unfold in a way that allows the assertion that the world is dominated by the scientific–technological Apparatus – that is, the fact that it occurs in the world, in relation to which one asserts that the Apparatus dominates the world – this fact is absolutely contingent, given that the occurrence of the world is an oc-curring onto what exists, originating from nothingness. The will to power is destined for the power of chance (and for the chance of power).

Certainly, when scientific consciousness happens to dwell on this line of thought, it immediately disposes of this by replying that the events of the world do not come from nothingness, but rather from a previous configuration of the world. Nevertheless, on the other hand, scientific consciousness is forced to acknowledge that the prior configuration of the world cannot *wholly* contain the new configuration: otherwise, there would be no transition from the previous to the new configuration, but rather a single static configuration. Science and, in general, present-day culture have not yet realized that the *novelty* of the new configuration is novelty *only* if the new has been nothing, that is, only if the new comes out of nothingness. If there were nothing, in the new, that was once nothing (if one were to exclude that every content and relationship forming the new was once nothing), then every content, form, aspect or relationship of events would have always existed, they would exist immutably. But such an immutable existence of the Whole is exactly what science and the entire culture aim to negate. In the most categorical way, the scientific consciousness and the historical consciousness of our time assert the processual, historical nature of reality; nonetheless, scientific consciousness and historical consciousness still leave buried in their unconscious the essential condition whereby reality is process and history: they hide in their unconscious the essential tie of things with being and with nothingness, which Ancient Greek philosophy brought to light once and for all, and according to which *the future is the nothingness from which things come* (and the past is the nothingness to which things return). What is essential and crucial in the way the current culture relates to the future still remains buried in the 'unconscious' of that culture. Yet, it is precisely such 'unconscious' – i.e. such unexpressed – that forms the essence of scientific–technological consciousness and of our entire culture.

12

The will to dominate wants what-is-to-be-dominated to exist, and that which is to be dominated in an absolute fashion ['l'assolutamente dominabile', t/n] is becoming, as understood by Ancient Greek ontology. However, the existence of becoming, which the will to power wants in order to be powerful, is also the extreme danger of the unpredictable, from which the will to power defends itself through prediction. The will for 'truth' – that is, the form of prediction around which the Western tradition is arranged – is *destined* to vanish into the form of prediction which is typical of scientific–technological rationality because such a second form of prediction frees becoming from the will for 'truth', which jeopardizes the nothingness of the future. Scientific prediction can *oc–cur* to be the most powerful form of domination (that is, the scientific domination of the world can be an *oc–currence*), only if science frees itself from the will for 'truth' that entifies nothingness.

Stating that Western civilization is *destined* to be a civilization of science and technics is not to express a prophecy: it is to exhibit that the history of the will to power is, in itself, the resolution ['toglimento', t/n] of a gigantic contradiction in which the nothingness of the future is forced to be a being. Therefore, saying that the fundamental tendency of our civilization is the progressive domination of the scientific–technological organization of existence, that is, the progressive affirmation of one of the two terms of the contradiction between the purposes of ideology and those of the scientific–technological Apparatus, means that this progressive domination of technics is not simply the occurrence of a fact but, indeed, the *destination* of the West for the civilization of technics. Asserting such a destination is not to make a prophecy which foresees that the fundamental tendency of our civilization will prolong into the future. The Western destination for the civilization of technics means that the scientific–technological Apparatus represents the negation, the resolution of the contradiction in which the will for 'truth' entifies the nothingness of the future, that is, entifies the nothingness from which things come from in the process of becoming. (And in the eyes of the Apparatus, the will for 'truth' is the supreme form of ideology.)

The perpetuation of this contradiction is undoubtedly possible. But its appearance and the appearance of its negation *indicate the direction* in which the other contradiction – i.e. the contradiction between the purposes of ideology and the purposes of the scientific–technological Apparatus, from which we started – is solved. They indicate the direction of the civilization of technics. And this indication is in fact the Western destination for the civilization of technics. The fundamental tendency of our civilization moves from the forgetfulness of the future to the acknowledgement that the future is the nothingness from which things come. Within this acknowledgement, science predicts and dominates the world.

But both science and the will for 'truth' are forms of the will to power, that is, of the *faith* in the *existence of becoming* (i.e. of what-is-to-be-dominated, of that which comes out of nothingness and returns to it). Only within this *faith* can one aim for world domination – and the civilization of technics is the most rigorous and powerful form of domination.

To grasp the essence of our civilization, then, should one not first of all peer into the abyss of this faith?

3

The ethics of science

1

The inevitable subordination of every purpose to the purpose that the scientific–technological Apparatus has in and of itself enlightens the meaning of what is nowadays called the 'ethics of science'.

'Ethics' is the acknowledgement that action is subject to constraints – no matter whether this acknowledgement comes from those who act or from a theoretical reflection that prescribes constraints on action (or describes an action that feels limited by constraints). At the beginning of the Western civilization, the principle emerged that knowledge has no constraints other than those imposed by the truth of knowledge itself. This principle stands in opposition to the biblical prohibition against tasting the fruits of the tree of knowledge. Therefore, even modern scientific knowledge only recognizes the constraints imposed by scientific rationality. The ethics of scientific knowledge is but the loyalty to the type of rationality expressed in science.

Yet science is not simply theoretical rationality: It is also the ability to transform the world, that is, it is technics. In fact, nowadays, science dominates the world not because it possesses the highest form of rationality; on the contrary, it is because the scientific domination of reality is now more powerful than any other form of domination that one can claim science that represents the highest form of rationality existing today. By now, science itself recognizes that its power over reality could suddenly vanish completely. This means that, in virtue of the configuration of scientific rationality, it is not possible to affirm the existence of a necessary link between such configuration and the power it exerts over reality. The theoretical greatness of science is exclusively measured by its capacity for domination.

However, with respect to science as the dominating power over the world, there arises the issue of establishing an ethical constraint to be something other than mere fidelity of science to its own type of rationality. Christianity, philosophy, politics, civil society, the state, liberal–democratic consciousness, the capitalist and communist worlds, and the various forms of humanism are the forces that have, over time, meant to determine what ethical constraints science should feel bound by, precisely because the scientific–technological activity has been regarded by such forces as the tool – nowadays the most effective one – for realizing what each of them considers the true purpose of human existence (see Chapter 2). In this context, the ethics of science consists in the subordination of science to the purpose proposed externally by these forces – a subordination where science functions as a means for achieving this purpose.

Nonetheless, the fact that these forces are in a conflictual relationship with each other; that, for each of them, the decisive tool for resolving the conflict in their favour is given, once again, by the extent of their control of the scientific–technological Apparatus; that real socialism and capitalism hold the monopoly over the production, use, and enhancement of the Apparatus, and that, in order to achieve their goals, both blocs are directly interested not only in the perpetuation but in the progressive enhancement of the Apparatus. This situation fosters the process where the *intrinsic* ethics of science gradually imposes itself over the others – that kind of ethics which is neither the simple fidelity of science to its own type of rationality, nor the subordination of science to purposes externally assigned to it. In effect, the intrinsic ethics of science is the will of science to realize the supreme purpose science has *in and of itself: the infinite increase* of its own power, the capacity to realize ever broader and more varied sets of purposes. Precisely because the Apparatus wants to dominate reality, there exists for it, in principle, no unbreakable limit to its domination and power; no degree of power is definitive and unsurpassable; and if the supreme goal of the Apparatus is the overcoming of every limit, the infinite expansion of its own power, then the Apparatus is currently simply bound by its own status as the supreme form of the will to power. That is, it is only bound by its will to dissolve every constraint.

The intrinsic ethics of science – the will to ever-increasing power ["la volontà di potere sempre di più", t/n] – is imposing itself on every other ethical force (Christianity, democracy, capitalism, communism, etc.) that has understood the Apparatus as a means for achieving its own goals; by aiming to take control of it and make it more and more powerful to use in the conflict against the opposing forces, it becomes unavoidable that non-scientific ethics themselves ultimately subordinate their specific aims to the intrinsic aim of the Apparatus, namely, the realization of the infinite increase of power. It becomes unavoidable that the Apparatus, from being a means, becomes the supreme end for those very forces that would want to use it as a means; it becomes unavoidable that, in the clash between capitalism and communism, the capitalist and communist values and goals end up being subordinated and sacrificed to the will to indefinitely increase the power of the tool that should make them materialize; it becomes unavoidable that such goals are subordinated to the infinite enhancement of the Apparatus, because either one of the two adversaries accepts that the power of the opponent is greater (which is equivalent to accepting the prevalence of the opponent's goals) or it decides, in turn, to pursue the strengthening of its own scientific–technological power at all costs: even at the expense of its own goals and ethics, should they turn out to be incompatible with the new level of power one decides to achieve. This is precisely why it was previously stated here that the conflict among non-scientific ethical forces facilitates the intrinsic ethics of the scientific–technological Apparatus: the indefinite increase of power.

Thus, a future is foreseeable where the opposition between capitalism and communism will no longer have any real content; that is, it will no longer be an opposition between capitalism and communism, but rather between two abstract, empty wills and ethics, each of which will simply want to seize or destroy the amount of power held by the other. Yet an even more distant future is foreseeable, where the Apparatus' will to indefinitely increase its own power will require the elimination of the residual opposition between those two abstract wills. That is, it will require the elimination of whatever prevents the boundless expansion of power. This is a future where the ethics of science will reign unchallenged across the planet. Exactly because this is the ethics of absolute creativity, it is also the ethics of absolute destructiveness: it destroys any state of the world that stands in the way of the indefinite increase of power.

Nor can our culture object, at this point, that the self-imposition of the intrinsic ethics of science destroys values that should not be destroyed. Indeed, if our culture, which currently leads every other culture on Earth, has come to reject all definitive truths, then even the attempt to save, against the ethics of science, the values of non-scientific ethics cannot claim to be a definitive truth. If no definitive truth exists, nothing remains but the conflict between forces on earth and the predominance of some over others. In fact, the scientific–technological Apparatus is the force that now dominates all others. To those who might retort that one does not need a definitive truth to detect and avoid evil and suffering, one should reply that the principle of avoiding evil and suffering is precisely one of those non-scientific ethical principles that presume to use science and technics but are ultimately destined to subordinate their characteristic goals to the increase of the Apparatus' power. Such an increase inevitably entails the manipulation of humanity and the amounts of suffering that comes with that. On the other hand, science cannot ignore the fact that humans do not want to suffer, just as it must consider all obstacles that delay the growth of its power. As a matter of fact, in this case, the obstacle is paramount, for the Apparatus is a social structure and the individuals who comprise it are not indifferent to the issue of human suffering.

The search for pleasure and the escape from pain can be considered a *fact* (therefore, the opposite fact could happen, as in the case of Nietzsche's 'overman', who does not reject pain and despises pleasure). In other words, such a fact cannot become a *principle* to be opposed to the infinite increase of power, that is, to a process that has the ability to become the most radical liberation from pain to have ever appeared. On the other hand, pleasures are followed by pains, and vice versa; and Plato, in the *Protagoras*, observes that to determine whether a pleasure should be enjoyed or rejected, it is necessary to incontrovertibly measure the chosen pleasure against the pain that follows it (or the rejected pain against the pleasure that would follow it). That is, the *epistéme*, the vision of incontrovertible truth, must become capable of measuring them, thus being, in fact, *metretiké epistéme* (*Protagoras* 357 b). From this measurement depends 'the salvation of life' (*e sotería toû bíou*, *Protagoras* 357 a): therefore, one can only rely on the incontrovertibility of *epistéme*. But the crisis of truth is the crisis of *epistéme* (and of the way in which the salvation of life is understood); therefore, no measurement can prove that avoiding a determinate suffering is preferable to preventing the increase in the power of the Apparatus. If this occurs *de facto*, it is because the social habits of countries managing the Apparatus are stronger than the will to realize such an increase through a certain amount of suffering, rather than through further refinement of technological possibilities.

2

In the history of the West, science is the highest form of the will to power. Yet, the way in which power is understood by Western culture, and therefore by modern science itself, leads to the exclusion of the idea of power as an 'objective fact' ['dato oggettivo', t/n], that is a real content that manifests itself, appearing in and of itself within experience.

In all the oldest human communities, power is something that is visible to all. The king, the leader, is the common reference point for the human group. It is precisely in relation to this common reference point that the human group becomes a *community*. This means that, already in the magical conception of the world, power is only such if it is no individual experience, but a social, public, communal one. The powerful one is not the one whose power remains unknown: rather, the powerful is the king, who is visible to everyone and shows his power to all. Nevertheless, such feature of power is not only typical of magic, but also of religion and science. Magic, religious faith, and science share not only the fact that they are specific ways to dominate the world: within them, the very concept of 'domination' is profoundly homogeneous. Indeed, domination is a social, public event; the larger the society that recognizes the existence of the domination, the more powerful the domination is. Domination tends to be recognized by the total society represented by humanity itself.

In Ancient Greek thought as well, domination and power are inseparable from their public, social, and intersubjective recognition. The Ancient Greek word *demiourgos*, which refers to God's creative activity, literally means 'they who work for the public' (or for the 'people', the *demos*), 'they who show their power publicly'. The divine power of the Demiurge is inseparable from its being recognized by the people of humankind. God's works are God's, that is, they are truly powerful, because everyone can see them. The Christian concept of the 'glory of God' expresses the same idea. The Latin word *gloria* alludes to that which can make itself heard, which is not closed off, but makes itself available for the listening of all. And even the Ancient Greek word *doxa*, which in the Vulgate is translated as *glory*, indicates that which is shown, manifested, that which is luminous and thus visible to all. The power of God is inseparable from the glory of God. For the *Brahmana of a hundred paths*, the sun would not rise if the minister did not offer the fire sacrifice. But Christ is the High Priest ['sommo sacerdote', t/n] who sacrifices himself so that the sun of salvation may rise for humanity. The ability to produce the salvation of humanity represents an even greater power than that which causes the sun to rise at dawn. Nonetheless, this supreme power requires the faith of humans, it demands to be recognized by all human beings. Faith is the eye through which the Glory of God shines. It is true that many do not believe in this world, but on the Day of Judgement, Christ will appear in his Glory. That is, everyone will see his power. The Day of Judgement is the supreme manifestation of God's power.

Thus, stating that nowadays the scientific–technological Apparatus subordinates all forms of power, which appeared throughout human history, means stating that the power of science receives a social recognition that is no longer afforded to magic, religion, politics, and so on. However, even for modern science, power over the world exists only if the totality of human groups acknowledges the existence of such power. Science is inseparable from its 'glory'. After all, a transformation of the world is deemed scientific only if it is perceived by all those who (according to scientific criteria) are considered sane. If the transformation of the world is only perceived by one individual or a minority group of individuals, science cannot grant it a scientific status. A world domination that people do not notice is not scientific. In explaining this concept C. S. Peirce, O. Neurath, and K. Popper, have repeated about science what modern science has always thought about itself: that domination and power are scientific only if they are not the content of a private experience, but enjoy public, social, and intersubjective recognition. Hence, it was no mere eccentricity when Popper stated that, if Robinson Crusoe had discovered and produced everything that was later discovered and produced by modern science on his deserted island, his entire discovery and creation would have had no scientific value, for they would have been realized within a private, individual experience, which would have remained outside the circle of social reaction to its establishment and presentation – the reaction that materializes as consent or dissent regarding the assertion of the existence and efficacy of that solitary work.

At this point, it is a matter of understanding that if power has a scientific character only if it is intersubjectively acknowledged, on the other hand, intersubjective recognition is no 'objective fact': it is not a content that is immediately given, manifest, evident in experience. On the contrary, the statement that intersubjective recognition exists is the result of an *interpretation*. That certain empirical events, immediately given in experience, *are* society and social recognition expressing themselves in language and behaviour; in other words, that there is a connection between some empirical events and meanings such as 'society' and 'social recognition' (where these concepts express the deeper meaning of those events); all this is not itself an empirical event immediately given in experience, but it is the result of *interpretation*, that is, of the will that – at the deepest and least controllable levels of our perception of the world – *establishes, decides* that the deeper meaning of those empirical events is expressed by those concepts. Although deeply rooted in human behaviour, however, interpretation indicates no necessary connections: It does not carry the value of definitive truth; and therefore, no matter how plausible the connections established by interpretation may be, the crucial ground upon which they are asserted is ultimately pure will, – i.e. pure faith, pure decision – that they exist. Interpretation is an interpreting will.

From these considerations it follows that if power has a scientific character only when it is publicly acknowledged, and if public recognition is not an immediately experienceable fact but indeed a result of the interpreting will, not even science's power over reality is an immediately experienceable fact but is itself something that the interpreting will wants and decides to exist. Something in which, through interpretation, one has faith.

The interpreting will is not something foreign to science: it belongs to the very essence of science, that is, to the essence of the scientific–technological Apparatus. Science requires public recognition of its power because at the root of the will to power, in which science consists, operates that kind of the originary form of the will to power, which is the interpreting will, i.e. the will that decides that a certain configuration of the world be the power, the domination, the success of science and of other forces contending for the world. Science *wants* domination, not only in the more familiar sense that domination is the goal science wants to achieve, but also in a much more radical and hidden sense: namely, it is the will to power itself that wants – decides, has faith – that the empirical datum ['il dato', t/n] produced by scientific action is the realization of the goals that such an action aims for. In other words, it is the will to power itself that, as an interpreting will, decides to interpret certain events as the public and, potentially, universal recognition of the dominance of science, and thus decides to believe that what exists today on earth is the dominance of science. Thus, not only does science want to dominate but it also decides for itself what the domination consists in – precisely because it is science itself, as an interpreting will, that decides that certain events are the public recognition of the domination of science (a recognition without which, for science, domination would lack any scientific character).[1]

Such a will, by which science decides that certain events should be understood as its domination over reality, is also present in religion. In the *Brahmana of the Hundred Paths*, one of humanity's greatest religious texts, it is said that 'the sun would not rise if the minister, at dawn, did not offer the fire sacrifice'. In this case too, *one decides* that a certain event – the rising of the sun – be the effect of the power of the sacrifice. Analogously, Christian consciousness *decides* that the salvation of humanity is the effect of the sacrifice of Jesus. Of course, science and religion have deeply different conceptual and practical structures; however, the power of science, like the power of religion, is not something directly observable in experience: Rather, it is the content of a faith – the faith in which the interpreting will consists.

It is an old way of understanding science to assert that the natural phenomena, which magic believes to produce, instead occur in accordance with the 'laws' of nature discovered through scientific investigation, and that only what is subject to these laws is truly real. In today's world, the so-called 'laws of nature' are grasped by science as 'hypotheses' that are kept until they are disproven by experience. And the experience, against which these hypotheses are measured, is not the individual, private experience, which could even conflict with the experience of others. The experience to which the hypotheses are compared, and which provides them with a scientific character, is the 'public opinion' – where the 'public' does not refer to a specific social or geographic area but, in principle, to all of humanity.

Science dominates and transforms the Earth. It has left behind all other forms of domination (brute force, magic, religion, politics, ideology). And for science, as has been shown, this domination has a scientific character and is the most powerful form of domination ever to appear, only insofar as there is no human community that does not show recognition of the existence of this domination. That is, only insofar as this existence is the object of the one, effective, irresistible 'universal consensus' nowadays present on earth. Without this consensus, science would not be science, and its power would be nought ['sarebbe nulla', t/n]. Yet it is certainly not because science 'objectively' dominates the world (nor because Robinson Crusoe 'objectively' dominates reality) that there exists universal consensus on the existence of this domination. On the contrary, it is because such a consensus exists that one can affirm that science 'objectively' dominates the world (and that Robinson Crusoe's domination is real). Therefore, the 'objective domination' is ultimately represented by the social recognition of that domination.

However – and this is again the crucial point – even the 'universal consensus' and 'social recognition' of the power of science are not 'objective data', immediately and directly attested in the human experience of the world. 'Consensus' and 'recognition' are human behaviours. Now, human behaviour is one of the most ambiguous, uncertain, unfathomable, and indecipherable aspects of reality. The simplest among human gestures, the briefest among human words are the most ambiguous. Even in relation to those who are closest to us, we can never be truly sure about what they meant to do or say. Often, each of us asks themselves this question even about themselves. Therefore, how infinitely *distant* is what we call 'the neighbour'! We often wonder whether the neighbour is like us. Yet after all, does 'the neighbour' really exist? Does that multiplicity of consciousnesses, which should be expressed or disguised in what we call 'the other's behaviour', truly exist? It seems that humanity has attempted to escape from this fundamental uncertainty, drawing maps, correcting them continually and constantly shifting reference points. It seems that for millennia humanity has believed to be able to catch glimpses of regularity in the unpredictability of human behaviour, thus venturing into the *interpretation* of 'the neighbour'. Nevertheless, despite every attempt and every refinement, our interpretation of the neighbour never becomes an evident and incontrovertible truth. This means that the conviction that a certain gesture or word is a sign of approval or disapproval, of consent or dissent, ultimately rests on *faith*, that is an *act of will*, a *decision*, an *interpretation*: the decision, the faith that that gesture or word is a sign of approval or disapproval, of consent or dissent.

Therefore, the idea that there is a universal consensus and universal social acknowledgement regarding the scientific domination of the Earth is not an 'objective fact', immediately and directly attested by experience: it is an *act of faith*, a *decision*, a will that the world has this meaning rather than another. Thus, one can claim that science dominates the world only because there exists a social recognition of that dominance. But the fact such recognition exists is not an evident truth, immediately attested by experience, but it is the content of a faith, an act of will, an interpretation, i.e. a decision that the world should have a certain meaning. Just as it is an interpretation, decision, faith, and will that the magical fire sacrifice causes the sun to rise, and that the sacrifice of Christ produces the salvation of humanity.

Scientific knowledge notices that the sun rises whether the priest performs the fire sacrifice or not, while atomic energy only develops in correlation with specific scientific–technological operations. But again, the power of atomic energy has a scientific character only if it is socially acknowledged; and the existence of this acknowledgement is not an objective fact, but the result of an interpretation. Then, with respect to the social acknowledgement of atomic energy, interpretation acts in a similar way to how it acts, in religious consciousness, with respect to the connection between the fire sacrifice and the rising of the sun.

It is undeniable that even magic and religion require, in addition to the faith in their contents, the faith in the existence of the social acknowledgement of their power; but even science requires, further to the faith in the existence of the social acknowledgement of its power, the faith that its conceptual apparatus has the ability to dominate the world. In other words, if science itself nowadays acknowledges that its dominance over the world could cease all of a sudden, this means that there exists no necessary connection between science's conceptual apparatus and the science's power over the world. And, therefore, that it is a faith that the fire sacrifice makes the sun rise (and that Christ's sacrifice saves humanity), just as it is a faith that the scientific conceptual apparatus dominates the world. In today's world, science itself excludes all definitive and incontrovertible truths. But if no truth exists, every belief stands at the same distance from the non-existent truth: at an infinite and impassable distance. According to this logic, one can no longer say that one faith is closer to truth than another, one can only say that one faith is more powerful than another. For example, the faith represented by science is more powerful than the faith of magic, religion, or of any other belief. And it is more powerful because the faith in the existence of a universal acknowledgement of the power of science is more powerful than any other faith.

One can observe that while faith does not question its own contents, science, on the other hand, adopts them hypothetically and is prepared to abandon them if experience disproved them or if a more explanatory hypothesis appeared. Undoubtedly, science formulates hypotheses. Yet this does in no way exclude that science, in its own power, relies on faith. Even though science does not believe in a necessary connection between its conceptual apparatus and its power over the world, science does *believe*, or *has faith*, that its current form of rationality enables a more effective domination of the world than could be achieved through all other conceptual apparatuses. In other words, even science has faith in the existence of a world to dominate and in its own ability to dominate it.

Therefore, not even science 'is' powerful: like magic, religion, and any form of domination, science 'decides', 'believes' that what happens is the effect of its power. Ultimately, the power of science is but the decision that its content be powerful. This decision defines our time. Our time is the time that has faith in the power of science and is sceptical of other forms of power. This does not mean that the faith of our time is 'more rational' – given that faith can only be more or less rational in relation to 'reason', that is, to the ability, to discern truth, which is denied in today's world. That is to say that the faith of our times is more powerful than the other faiths – in the sense that the faith in the greater power of science is, at the same time, faith in the greater power of this faith. Undoubtedly, on the other hand, will does not interpret arbitrarily, but consistently with rules (which are not absolutely binding though). After all, it is precisely by aligning itself with its own rules that the interpretive will can affirm that the power of the scientific–technological Apparatus nowadays dominates every other form of power. With a certain degree of regularity, certain events occur in conjunction with scientific action; and they are regularly associated with another group of events, which, in the eyes of the interpretive will, coincide with the public acknowledgement that the first group of events is the realization of the goals of science, that is, the expression of the power of science over the world and over other forms of power. In other words, it is by aligning with its own rules that the interpretive will can assert that the object of public acknowledgement is the power of science and no longer the power of religion, magic, or any other cultural form.

At the root of the scientific–technological Apparatus' will to indefinitely increase its power – that is, at the root of the ethics of science – lies the interpretive will, the will to give the world a certain meaning. According to this meaning, the world appears to be dominated by science. This does not mean ignoring the 'objective', experienceable ['sperimentabile', t/n] dimension given by the regularities, with which the events usually said to be 'produced' by scientific action occur. It means emphasizing that such regularities have scientific value (i.e. intersubjective value) only within the interpretive will, that is, within the belief that the world has a certain meaning.

3

But at the root of the will to power operates something even deeper than the faith in the existence of scientific domination. As a matter of fact, the will to power can want to dominate, to indefinitely expand its dominance, and have faith in the existence of its dominance only if, first and foremost, it *wants* what-is-to-be-dominated to exist. Now, what-is-to-be-dominated is the world's becoming. One can intend to dominate reality only if *one believes* that reality is becoming, time, history: that its order and configuration are temporary and dissoluble. The *newer* what comes to be ['sopraggiunge', t/n], and the farther what ceases to be ['si allontana', t/n], the more intense and radical the process of becoming is. For the first time, Ancient Greek philosophy thought that what is radically new is what used to be *nothing*, and that what is brought to an extreme distance from existence is what comes to be *nothing* again. For the first time, becoming appears as the coming out of nothingness and returning into nothingness. The faith in the existence of becoming is the dimension within which all of Western civilization comes to light. Even though science tends to disregard its philosophical roots, every language and practice of science has a hidden depth far beyond what science itself is aware of. It is *ontology*, that is, the Ancient Greek reflection on the meaning of being and nothingness, that is the depth which gives meaning to the language and practice of science.

Therefore, in Western civilization, the will to power is possible only as grounded in the faith in the existence of becoming, which is what Ancient Greek thought meant by the word *becoming*. Indeed, the faith in the existence of the world's becoming is the originary form of the will to power. The will to power of the West, which culminates in the will to power of the scientific-technological Apparatus, reaches its extreme radicality in that it is the Ancient Greek meaning of becoming that reaches ultimate radicality. On the basis of the Ancient Greek meaning of becoming, science wants to endlessly increase its ability to create and annihilate orders and worlds, that is, to make them come out of nothing and return to nothing. The foundation of the ethics of science is the faith in the existence of becoming, i.e. the originary form of the will to power.

This faith is the foundation of all Western ethics. However, while every Western ethical tradition has sought to impose an immutable order, which ultimately makes the faith in becoming impossible – something that the West, since its beginnings, has felt as the highest self-evidence – the ethics of science, on the contrary, is the negation of any immutable order, because it is the will to indefinitely increase its own power (that is, its capacity to transform any arrangement in the world). Thus, in the history of the West, this will for infinite growth of power represents the ultimate fidelity to the faith in becoming, that is, in the sense of becoming brought to light by Ancient Greek philosophy.

In Western culture, this faith is lived as the highest self-evidence and, at the same time – especially in scientific culture – it is considered something one can completely disregard. When this faith is lived as the highest self-evidence, one objects that becoming, the coming out of nothing and returning to it, is not the content of a faith or a will, but something given in and of itself and independent of will. Nevertheless, the meaning and the incontrovertibility of this given ['dato', t/n] and this independence from the will have never been questioned. The critical sense of Western culture has questioned everything yet always remaining within the conviction that reality, with which humans engage, comes out of nothing and returns to nothing. In other words, that it is historical, temporal, perishable, contingent, becoming. This conviction has never been questioned. Therefore, removed from any problematization, it is but faith, the Western fundamental faith. It is interpretation, the fundamental interpretation, upon which all other interpretations are based and, thus, also the interpretation according to which certain events are the public acknowledgement of the power of science (the interpretation that decides that the power of science is real, i.e. decides what such power consists in).

However, as often happens in scientific knowledge, when one believes to have nothing to do with the Ancient Greek meditation on the meaning of nothingness, being, and becoming, the Ancient Greek faith in becoming becomes even more dominant. For by disregarding meditation, one of the essential conditions for it being questioned vanishes. The scientific concepts of 'time', 'becoming', 'process', 'variation', 'change', 'production', 'destruction', 'innovation' have no meaning outside the interpretation of becoming in terms of 'nothingness' and 'being'. Disregarding these terms simply intensifies their dominance over the language and practice of science.

Therefore, the decisive issue in today's thinking concerns the meaning and value of the Ancient Greek faith and interpretation of becoming. By questioning this faith, one questions the very essence of our civilization. And also: if the Ancient Greek faith in becoming is the foundation of the ethics of science, that is, the will to indefinitely increase its power, questioning the Ancient Greek faith and interpretation of the world's becoming means, for the first time, seriously questioning the ethics of science itself.

4

Élenchos

1

Science starts turning to morality but finds itself facing a disappearing shadow. Science asks how far it must submit to moral laws; ethics has become incapable of showing their value. Sensitivity to the destructive aspects of science and technics grows, yet it has never been so uncertain whether the unacceptability of destruction is something more than the will of certain human groups not to be destroyed or not to destroy. The more the existence of moral constraints is known and considered on the planet, the more the ability to justify those constraints decreases – within the culture that develops within the fundamental faith of the West.

The crisis of philosophy is the crisis of ethics. On one hand, attempts to save ethics from the shipwreck of philosophy realize that the construction of a 'scientific ethics' results in the identification of 'factual judgements' and 'value judgements', and on the other hand, that the distinction between these two kinds of judgements has become problematic. Indeed, 'evaluation' belongs to scientific knowledge itself. Evaluation is not the acknowledgement of the existence of a value, but the will for something to have value, that is, ultimately, it is the pure will to want something.

Nonetheless, the problematic character of the distinction between fact and value manifests itself particularly in an unexplored dimension: that of science's will to indefinitely increase its dominance over the world, and of the need to consider the existence of this dominance as the result of an interpretation. 'Scientific ethics' can only be the intrinsic ethics of science, that is, the will to increase power indefinitely and the subordination of all other forms of ethics to this will. Yet, when in contemporary culture an attempt is made to construct a 'scientific ethics', one is deluded into thinking that scientific knowledge can establish the existence of ethical constraints that limit the will to indefinitely expand the power of the scientific–technological Apparatus.

In recent years, a movement has developed in Anglo-Saxon countries and Germany to save ethics from the shipwreck of philosophy, while avoiding the path of 'scientific ethics'. At the centre of this attempt is the rejection of philosophy as a foundational knowledge that rests on 'first' (or 'ultimate') principles, and the proposal of a philosophy and of a 'foundation' of morality grasped as a 'reconstructive' knowledge that brings to light the 'inevitable presuppositions' *of every* meaningful linguistic action. This attitude is reflected in philosophers like R. S. Peters, K. O. Apel, A. J. Watt, and J. Habermas.

The fundamental attitude of these philosophers is decisively critical of philosophy's claim to know incontrovertible and definitive truths; yet, the determination of the inevitable presuppositions of every meaningful linguistic action revives one of the most distinctive figures of classic philosophy – in fact, if one considers this from the perspective of the 'foundation' of knowledge, it brings back what, for classic philosophy, is undoubtedly *the* fundamental figure of the structure of knowledge: the *élenchos*, that is, the 'refutation' directed at those who, wishing to reject certain meanings or assertions, are inevitably forced to accept them in order to reject them.

If the *élenchos* is the fundamental figure of classic thought, it is also the least explored in the reflection in which philosophy today engages around that thought. The discussion of the meaning and scope of *élenchos* is the foundation of all my writings. *The Originary Structure* specifically refers to the opening of meaning, that is, the semantic structure that is necessarily presupposed by every form of knowledge, and therefore also by that form which is the very negation of that structure – so that such negation, denying that which it cannot be without (i.e. its 'foundation'), becomes a self-negation.[1] Indeed, the originary structure is 'originary' because the negation (any negation) of it appears originarily (i.e. in virtue of its semantic content) as self-negation.[2]

Plato uses the word *élenchos* both to refer to the attempt to refute what cannot be refuted (see, for example, *Sophist*, 238 d) and to indicate the refutation that affects and imposes itself on those who believe they can deny something that cannot be denied (see, for example, *Sophist*, 252 c). Those who intend to 'refute' (*elénchein*) non-being by saying that *it* is neither unity nor plurality, that one cannot state *it*, think it, and that it is unutterable, unsayable ['indicibile', t/n], ineffable, and meaningless (*Sophist*, 238c), must recognize that they are talking about it, thinking about it, expressing it, thus treating it as a being, and that therefore, their attempt to 'refute' non-being resolves itself in an 'aporia', that is, in a 'self-contradiction' (*enantía ... légein*, 238 d). Non-being cannot be expelled from thinking and from the sayable ['dicibile', t/n], because such an expulsion presupposes the thinkability and sayability ['dicibilità', t/n] themselves of non-being.

But there is also the *élenchos*, the 'refutation' of those who believe they can deny something undeniable. For instance, those who reject any synthesis (*koinonía*) of different determinations ['determinatezze', t/n] are 'refutable' by their own rejection, because the rejection of any synthesis of different entities is itself expressed in a thought and language that is a synthesis of differences (*Sophist*, 252 c). In the previous case, the term *élenchos* referred to the negation that pretends to eliminate the truth; now, the term *élenchos* refers to the negative movement that eliminates the negation of truth.

It is in such a second sense that Aristotle uses the term *élenchos* in the Book IV of the *Metaphysics*: To 'demonstrate negatively' (*apodeîxai ... elenktikôs*, 1006 a 11–12), that it is impossible to deny the *principium firmissimum* (that is, what will later be called the 'principle of non-contradiction').[3] This principle asserts that the content of thinking is determinate; but those who deny this principle think, with their denial, something determinate. That is, their denial of the principle, in order to emerge, must inevitably presuppose what it intends to deny. The *élenchos* is precisely the acknowledgement of this inevitable presupposition.

The philosophers mentioned earlier (Peters, Apel, Watt, Habermas) believe they can show that those who deny the more general and formal ethical norms must inevitably presuppose them, and therefore contradict themselves. They acknowledge (for example, Apel and Habermas) their debts to Descartes' *cogito ergo sum*, but they do not do the same with Aristotle's *élenchos* or even with Plato's. Descartes' *cogito* can be expressed as the awareness that, in the very act of denying my existence, I acknowledge (with this very denial) that I exist.

They also recognize their debts to the 'minimal logic' (which, in Popper's school, is considered the logical area present in any thinking being), to the conceptual apparatus underlying our experience (itself irreplaceable, as P. F. Strawson notes, because it is present in alternative apparatuses as well), and to Kant's transcendental conditions of experience (also considered irreplaceable, and therefore as inevitable presuppositions). But in all these cases, the level of the discourse remains below that of Aristotle, for it simply underscores that, since those who deny certain conceptual structures are forced to accept them, they contradict themselves; while Aristotle's *élenchos* refers to the denial of the impossibility of self-contradiction and highlights that anyone who denies this impossibility, with this denial and in this very denial, affirms it. In other words, Aristotle takes into account the *originary dimension* of the inevitable presuppositions of what one intends to deny; all others are more or less derived dimensions.

Habermas suggests a 'more cautious version' of the 'transcendental–pragmatic' foundation of ethics, constructed by K. O. Apel – who in turn draws on the studies of R. S. Peters and J. Hintikka. It is a 'non-deductive' foundation of the most general and fundamental ethical norms. In other words, it excludes the possibility that these norms may be deduced from 'first' (or 'ultimate') principles and aims to show that every individual, and therefore even the moral sceptic, not only inevitably presupposes a 'minimal logic' but also presupposes, by the very fact of participating in the discussion, certain fundamental ethical norms; and thus – when, like the sceptic, they deny them – they contradict themselves. The foundation of such norms is precisely the identification of this contradiction, and therefore, their acceptance would not be attributable to a simple social convention.

2

Nevertheless, with all these philosophers, the rejection of contradiction essentially rests on the way in which Popper himself rejects contradiction. Popper rejects it because 'if two contradictory assertions are admitted, any assertion must be admitted', which would lead to the 'radical failure of science', the 'collapse of science' (*Conjectures and Refutations, What is dialectic?*). That is to say that anyone who does not care about this collapse or failure is allowed to continue contradicting themselves and therefore to continue to deny the ethical norms they presuppose as participants in the discussion.

On the other hand, Popper himself asserts that the genuinely rationalistic attitude – i.e. the significance attributed to argumentation and experience – cannot be proven through arguments or experience. He means that the genuinely rationalistic attitude is adopted in virtue of 'an irrational *faith* in reason' (*The Open Society and Its Enemies*, XXIV, 2).[4] Yet according to Popper, the principle of non-contradiction is precisely something without which science, that is, reason, could not exist. Thus, the rejection of contradiction is an 'irrational faith' in non-contradiction.

Thus, anyone attempting, following Popper, to refute the sceptic who denies all moral norms, because the sceptic contradicts themselves, must resign themselves to considering their refutation as an 'irrational faith' in morality – which is the exact opposite of what Popper means to achieve through a transcendental–pragmatic foundation of moral principles (even to the extent of not agreeing with the possibility of an 'ultimate foundation').

In other words, these authors, engaged in finding a middle path between scepticism and absolute foundation, focus all their attention on the contradiction in which the denier of any moral norms finds themselves. Yet these authors fail to notice that their concept of 'non-contradiction' transforms their refutation of the sceptic into a simple 'irrational faith' in the need to abandon the sceptical stance. While Popper acknowledged that the choice of a rationalistic attitude is a 'moral decision' (*op. cit.*, XXIV, 3), these authors unsuccessfully attempt to show that moral principles are rational because they are presupposed by all those who participate in the dialogical dimension of the discussion.

This failure is due not only to the fact that, by ignoring the meaning of Aristotle's *élenchos*, they end up with a mere faith in non-contradiction, but it is also due to the way they develop the thesis according to which the first moral principles are presupposed by anyone who accepts dialogue.

Properly speaking, for Apel and Habermas, dialogue is the 'community' described by Peirce and Mead, where the unlimited process of communication between human beings unfolds. 'Participants in argumentation', Habermas writes, 'cannot avoid the presupposition that [...] the structure of their communication rules out all external or internal coercion other than the force of the better argument and thereby also neutralizes all motives other than that of the cooperative search for truth'.[5] This search is a 'competition' to build the 'better arguments' (*op. cit.*, p. 88). Those who participate in this competition must follow certain rules. For example, each person must say what they believe, not what they are forced to say without believing it; everyone must allow those who are capable to speak and must not force them to say what they do not intend to say; every statement must be open to questioning. In other words, these rules prescribe the *equality* of participants in the competition and their *freedom* of opinion (i.e. the rejection of any repression that forces them to behave differently from how they wish). But these rules are the same fundamental principles of morality. Therefore, anyone participating in the argument 'inevitably presupposes' these principles. Hence, when the sceptic who participates in the argument denies these principles, they deny what they inevitably presuppose. That is, they contradict themselves. The analytical complications introduced by Habermas concern the description of the inevitable presuppositions of argumentation – and here it can be conceded that such a description is impeccable.

Yet, there remains a *presupposition*, at the core of Habermas' discourse (and of his followers), a presupposition that is *his* (and theirs) and therefore not an inevitable presupposition. This lies in conceiving of the dialogical and intersubjective dimension of argumentation as an *objective fact*, as a *given reality*, a structure of the world existing independently of any critical reflection on it – the presupposition that has been repeatedly mentioned in the previous pages.

Once again, Popper's influence is crucial. According to Popper, Kant was the first to show that every 'perception' is an 'interpretation'. The 'data' of experience are 'interpretations carried out in the light of theories, and therefore affected by the hypothetical and conjectural character of every theory' (*Conjectures and Refutations*, Addenda, 1).[6] On one hand, Popper is engaged in defending this thesis (whose weight in Nietzsche's thought seems to be overlooked by Popper) against empiricism and neo-positivism, while also supporting that the 'impartial judge' of any scientific controversy is 'public opinion', i.e. the social, intersubjective dimension. *On the other hand*, Popper does not realize that the existence of the dialogical, public, intersubjective dimension is itself something *interpreted*, that is, it is no immediate fact attested by experience.

Besides, interpreting itself cannot be understood as an objectively existing intersubjective function: Rather, interpreting is the will to give a meaning to the world. And intersubjectivity belongs to this meaning, it is a part of it. Yet for Popper – and later for Apel, Habermas and others – the social dimension is an objectively existing reality, a fact ['dato', t/n], the existence of which is not something interpreted but incontrovertible. Thus, the affirmation of the existence of the social dimension is a *theory*, which, even being hypothetical and conjectural like any other theory, is not questioned. Therefore, it is not an inevitable presupposition for those participating in the argument, but an *arbitrary* presupposition, exempt from criticism.

The sceptic can then raise an objection that Habermas does not foresee. Suppose – the sceptic might say – that certain normative contents are inevitable presuppositions of argumentation. Nevertheless, one can participate in the public dimension of argumentation knowing that the existence of that dimension is the result of an interpretation, that is, of a hermeneutical faith or hypothesis. Those normative contents are binding *within* that faith or hypothesis. If one participates in public argumentation, one is thus bound; but that such an argumentation exists (and that there exists something like 'participating in such an argumentation') is not binding. Thus, the moral principles inevitably presupposed by argumentation can be questioned, precisely by questioning the existence of the intersubjective dimension belonging to the argumentation. In other words, *without contradicting themselves*, the sceptic can question and deny the moral principles inevitably presupposed by argumentation.

Certainly, Habermas too joins that 'paradigm shift' that leads 'pragmatism' and 'hermeneutic philosophy' to abandon 'the justificatory and self-justificatory claims' of the philosophy of consciousness from Kant to Hegel: 'Pragmatism and hermeneutics oust the traditional notion of the solitary subject that confronts objects and becomes reflective only by turning itself into an object. In its place they put an idea of cognition that is mediated by language and linked to action. Moreover, they emphasize the web of everyday life and communication surrounding 'our' cognitive achievements'. Essentially, this web coincides with 'common sense' (*op. cit.*, p. 9). But acknowledging the existence of common sense and conceiving of philosophy as 'reconstructive science' (or 'universal pragmatics') that makes explicit the rules, according to which common sense is formed, does not mean one is authorized to transform into truth the beliefs of common sense. Thus, one is not authorized to transform into truth the beliefs affirming the reality of the social and intersubjective dimension.

In addition, the philosophy of consciousness can reply that the 'subject' is not 'solitary' because it is the transcendental consciousness of every content, and thus also of common sense and of the intersubjective linguistic dimension. In this case, scepticism is an ally of transcendental consciousness, which sees the problematic nature of its content and thus also of the moral principles belonging to it. In this direction, the philosophy of consciousness developed in Gentile's actualism and Ugo Spirito's problematicism. But then, the assertion that knowledge is 'mediated by language' can only mean that non-linguistic contents *never appear*, in fact, separate from the language that expresses them – where this presence is the openness ['l'apertura', t/n] without which one could not even speak of language.

After what has been said about the objection – not foreseen by Habermas – that the sceptic can raise against the attempt to show that moral principles are inevitable presuppositions of argumentation, the objection raised by Habermas *is cut off* from the transcendental–pragmatic foundation of morality proposed by Apel, which resides precisely in the identification of the inevitability of those presuppositions.

Popper had observed that the irrationalist 'can always refuse to accept arguments, either all arguments or those of a certain kind', and that 'such an attitude can be carried through without becoming logically inconsistent' (*The Open Society and Its Enemies*, XXIV, 2). On one hand, Habermas intends to show, surpassing Apel's result, that the sceptic (i.e. the irrationalist) can, as

Popper said, refuse to participate in the discussion (thus freeing themselves from the contradiction, attributed to them by Apel, of having to presuppose what they deny); and on the other hand, Habermas intends to show that, notwithstanding this, such a last move of the sceptic is doomed to failure because, being a type of rejection, it is again a way of presupposing what it rejects.

Let us say that this 'objection' from the sceptic – the refusal to participate in the discussion – is ['rimane', t/n] excluded (and therefore Habermas' reply to this objection is also excluded) because there exists a more radical and more 'consistent' scepticism than the one Habermas envisions (this scepticism intends to prevail over the 'consistent sceptic', that is, the sceptic who has freed themselves as much as possible from inconsistency). Authentically radical scepticism is not the one that refuses to participate in the discussion, but – as has been seen – it is the one that asserts the problematic nature of the existence of the intersubjective dimension of the discussion.

Nonetheless, in line with Popper, Habermas notes that a sceptic who 'sees in advance that he will be caught in performative contradictions [those in which, in order to deny a statement, one must presuppose it] will reject the game of wits from the outset', positioning themselves in the 'dropout posture of the sceptic' or depriving 'the transcendental pragmatist of a basis for his argument'. Yet, for Habermas, rationalism can avoid the 'residue of decisionism', which, although he does not explicitly say it, refers to Popper's irrational faith in reason, that is, the (non-arguable) *will* to argue.

Indeed, Habermas states that

> By refusing to argue, for instance, he cannot, even indirectly, deny that he moves in a shared sociocultural form of life, that he grew up in a web of communicative action, and that he reproduces his life in that web. In a word, the sceptic may reject morality, but he cannot reject the ethical substance (*Sittlichkeit*) of the life circumstances in which he spends his waking hours,

not unless he is willing to take refuge in suicide or serious mental illness. In other words, he cannot extricate himself from the communicative practice of everyday life in which he is continually forced to take a position by responding yes or no. As long as he is still alive *at all*, a Robinson Crusoe existence through which the sceptic demonstrates mutely and impressively that he has dropped out of communicative action is inconceivable, even as a thought experiment.

'That is why the radical sceptic's refusal to argue is an empty gesture. No matter how consistent a dropout he may be, he cannot drop out of the communicative practice of everyday life, to the presuppositions of which he remains bound. And these in turn are at least partly identical with the presuppositions of argumentation as such'. (For this citation and for the last ones, see Habermas, *Moral Consciousness and Communicative Action*, p. 100–1).[7]

The substance of Habermas' argument is that, simply by remaining alive – and by not committing suicide or falling into serious mental illness – the sceptic must presuppose what they deny. In other words, the sceptic must presuppose certain assertive and normative contents, which represent the conditions for the dimension itself of argumentation, into which they believe they can refuse participation. Nonetheless, according to Habermas, the suicidal sceptic appears to be 'consistent', that is, their rejection of moral principles can be carried out without contradiction, if they refuse, by committing suicide, to participate in the discussion. (This cannot be said for 'serious mental illness' if it consists in the inability to think: in that case, there is no longer even a sceptic.)

But apart from this circumstance, even assuming that the sceptic cannot 'drop out' from life as long as they remain a sceptic, this does not in any way mean they must live by accepting the presuppositions of the discussion, that is, the presuppositions consisting in recognizing the equality and freedom of opinions of the participants in the discussion. What one is forced to presuppose cognitively as long as one participates in life does not necessarily include, in fact almost never includes, what one is forced to presuppose cognitively when participating in the discussion as a 'contest' where the only 'coercion' is the best argument. In life, the best argument is never the winning coercion. Thus, the presuppositions of daily praxis, of which the sceptic remains a prisoner, are almost *never* 'identical with the presuppositions of argumentation as such'. The sceptic may exercise their violence on others – and deny, in addition to morality, ethical life – and their rejection of argumentation will not at all be 'an empty gesture'. The entire history of the world is made up of this 'consistent' violence. A consistent sceptic is therefore not only the suicidal one, but simply every oppressor.

3

Habermas' argument, which is untenable for the transcendental–pragmatic foundation of moral principles, reprises a renowned Aristotelian case against the sceptic – the universal sceptic, not just the sceptic with respect to moral principles. The universal sceptic is one who denies the distinction between determinations, that is, they deny the principle of non-contradiction. Aristotle (even in this case, not mentioned by Habermas) says that even such a sceptic does not truly think that determinations are not different from one another: 'For why does a man walk to Megara and not stay at home, when he thinks he ought to be walking there? Why does he not walk early some morning into a well or over a precipice, if one happens to be in his way?' (*Metaph.*, IV, 1008 b 14–17).

Aristotle alludes exactly to the scenario where the universal sceptic, simply by virtue of living, acknowledges what they intend to deny (that is, they acknowledge the difference of determinations). This is the pragmatic variant of Aristotle's *élenchos*. The fundamental form of the *élenchos* consists in highlighting the determinacy of the *discourse* that intends to deny determinacy (that is, the identity of the determination with itself and its being other than other determinations). On the other hand, the pragmatic variant of the *élenchos* consists in observing that the *way of life* of the one who denies determinacy makes it seem as though they recognize and accept determinacy (e.g. going to Megara as different from not going there). Nevertheless, the solidity ['consistenza', t/n] of these two figures of the *élenchos* is very different.

Firstly, because the pragmatic variant observes that the way of life of the denier of determinacy *makes it seem*, in fact, that they acknowledge determinacy. Aristotle says that this acknowledgement is something 'evident', 'manifest' (*phanerón*, 1008b 12; *phaínetai*, 1008b 16; *dêlon*, 1000b 18); yet, it is not evident because from the sceptic's behaviour – their avoidance of jumping into the well – one can only *infer, presume, interpret* that for the sceptic, falling and not falling into the well are not the same thing and that, therefore, they too acknowledge the determinacy of determinations. This interpretation can be replaced by an infinite number of others though: that is, like any interpretation, it has a problematic value. It is therefore problematic whether the sceptic acknowledges, by living, what they deny; in other words, the pragmatic variant of the Aristotelian *élenchos* has a problematic character. And because the 'certainty' of the 'most certain of all principles' (*bebaiotáte arché*, Metaph., 1005b 11–12) cannot be separated from the *élenchos*, the pragmatic variant of this undermines the certainty of the certain principle.

Secondly, even if the problematic interpretation of the sceptic's behaviour were to become something evident and incontrovertible – that is, if it were evident that the sceptic does not think that jumping and not jumping into the well are the same – the sceptic could reply by saying that it is simply their will to survive, their instinct, that forces them to regard jumping and not jumping into the well as different, and that this will and instinct are not to be confused with the *truth*, and that 'truth' is the mask behind which the instinct for survival hides and protects itself. In fact, Nietzsche's criticism of the Aristotelian principle of non-contradiction is fully valid with regards to the pragmatic variant of the *élenchos* (even though Nietzsche does not analytically consider the *élenchos* and even less distinguishes its various forms).

That is to say that the sceptic may acknowledge their inability *de facto* to 'drop out' from the acknowledgement of determinacy – an incapacity produced by various reasons, not least the will to survive and to make the world liveable. Yet the sceptic does not acknowledge truth in their idiosyncrasies. Just as they do not recognize truth in the idiosyncrasy of acknowledging the presuppositions accepted by participating in a discussion, or in the presuppositions accepted simply by living.

However, against the sceptic who refuses to be refuted by the pragmatic variant of the *élenchos*, Aristotle can oppose the fundamental form of the *élenchos*. This form succeeds in refuting the sceptic (i.e. the one who identifies the different), showing that they recognize what they deny, i.e. the determinacy of determinations (the difference of the different). In effect, when the sceptic *distinguishes* their idiosyncrasies from truth, they are precisely acknowledging the difference of the different that they want to deny. Or also: by distinguishing between their (and others') idiosyncrasies (affirmation of differences) and what is true (the nullification of differences), the sceptic does not intend to express another of their idiosyncrasies: they intend to express the truth itself, and since this truth is determinate, the sceptic accepts what they believe to be denying. If then, the sceptic were to argue that their discourse (that is, their denial of the principle of non-contradiction) is nothing but an idiosyncrasy, then they would no longer be a denier of truth and of the most certain principle of all.

On the other hand, it is undeniable that the Aristotelian *élenchos* – both in its fundamental form and in its pragmatic variant – refers to an intersubjective situation. In effect, the *élenchos* is the *discourse* by which an individual in possession of true *logos* and the consciousness of this truth ('the philosopher', 1005b 11) refutes thinking individuals who believe they can deny this truth.

The Aristotelian *élenchos* presents itself as a linguistic relationship between different consciousnesses. Thinking ['il pensiero', t/n] is always – true or false – the thinking of 'someone' (*tís*, 1005b 26); the *élenchos* is the refutation 'of another' (*állou*, 1006a 17), i.e. of *the one* who denies the first principle, and consists in *asking* them what meaning their statement has: 'interrogated ... they must answer' (*eroménou ... apokritéon*, 1007a 12–13); and in this 'dialogue' (*dialegésthai*, Metaphysics, 20) one can *say* to them that they presuppose what they deny. The *élenchos* exists ['sussiste', t/n] because, 'if the denier of the principle says something' (*eàn mónon ti légei*, 1006a 12–13). And the denier of the principle, who does not go to Megara and does not throw themselves into the well, is again an individual different from the 'philosopher'. The Platonic 'dialogue' is the grand precursor of the intersubjective dialogical situation of the Aristotelian *élenchos*.

Yet again, the very subsistence of this situation is problematic. Only within *faith*, that is, within the *interpreting will*, can one think that the denial of truth is incarnated in a denier of truth and in a language in which it is expressed; in a consciousness different from the one represented by the actual appearing ['l'apparire attuale', t/n]. Plato and Aristotle (and, as we are seeing, many others, even today) remain within this faith. That something is language, that this language expresses the denial of truth, that this denial is thought by a consciousness different from the actual appearing of the world, that certain events called 'my language' are my dialogue with my 'neighbour'; all of this is not phenomenologically manifest, but it is the content of the interpreting will (faith) – even if this will, on its part, is manifest, appears and is phenomenologically detectable. (What does not appear is the content of faith, but faith – having faith, wanting certain events to have a certain meaning – appears.) Hence, even the fundamental form of the Aristotelian *élenchos* is inscribed in a hypothetical structure: *if* the intersubjective content affirmed by the interpretation exists, *then* the denier of the non-contradictoriness of being acknowledges and affirms what they intend to deny.

Yet, at the same time, the Aristotelian *élenchos is distinguished* from the very hypothetical structure in which it is inscribed, in the sense that the dialogical relationship between 'the philosopher', that is, the individual who possesses true *logos*, and the individual who denies the truth, *differs* from the relationship between truth and the denial of truth. Independently of any intersubjective situation, even in such denial it is evident that the denial of the determinacy (i.e. non-contradictoriness) of being subsists only as it is a form of the acknowledgement and affirmation of determinacy. This 'dialogue' between truth and its own negation belongs to the essence of truth.[8] It is at this point – that is, when the Aristotelian *élenchos* is considered in its capacity to differ from its dialogical–intersubjective context – that the discussion on the *élenchos*, as is developed in *The Essence of Nihilism*, begins.

Nihilism is the belief in the existence of becoming. In this belief lies the true meaning of nihilism. What nihilism in truth is can appear only if the *truth* appears. Truth is none of the 'truths' of the West (or of the East). Yet, truth is the relationship between truth and its own negation. Truth is the negation of its own negation, precisely because the negation of truth is what it is, only insofar as it is an *affirmation* of truth. The negation of truth is self-negation. The originary structure of truth is exactly the appearing of the self-negation of the negation of truth. The determinate content, which is negated by the negation of truth, is the appearing of beings, where beings (the positive) appear as not being their own other ['nel suo non essere il proprio altro', t/n] (i.e. the negative, represented both by the other beings and by nothingness). The opposition between the positive and the negative (this opposition is precisely the determinacy of the positive) is originarily united with the appearing of the positive. This originary unity is the originary structure of truth. The Aristotelian *élenchos* indicates that the denial of the opposition between the positive and the negative is a positive that stands in opposition to ['si oppone al', t/n] its own negative, i.e. it is a determinate being. The negation of determinacy 'inevitably presupposes' its own determinacy. And the determinacy of the negation of the opposition is the determinacy of the relation in which non-opposition consists, that is, the identity of the positive and the negative, and therefore it is the determinacy of both the positive and the negative. The determinacy of the negation of opposition is the determinacy of the elements that form such negation.

All this does not mean that the Aristotelian *élenchos* shows the incontrovertibility of nihilism. The *élenchos* shows the impossibility of negating the determinacy of beings. However – one might observe – given that the beings that Aristotle speaks of are both the becoming being and the immutable being, it follows that the *élenchos* shows the impossibility of negating that determinacy which is the determinacy of the becoming beings ['dell'ente diveniente', t/n], that is, those beings forming the content of the faith in the existence of becoming – the faith which represents the true meaning of nihilism.

Nevertheless, this conclusion is unacceptable, for it is necessary that the negation of determinacy be a determinacy, but this necessity *does not equate* to the necessity that the determinacy presupposed by the negation of determinacy be represented by the determinacy of becoming beings. The *configuration* of the determinate (its being either immutable or becoming) is not established by the *élenchos* as such (that is, as the detection that the negation of the determinate is a determinate), but by the nihilistic (pre)conception ['(pre)comprensione', t/n] of being, within which the Aristotelian *élenchos* functions. If on one hand, the Aristotelian *élenchos inherits* the configuration of the determinate from this understanding, on the other hand, the detection that the negation of determinacy inevitably presupposes determinacy alludes to determinacy *as such*, and not to determinacy as the determinacy of the immutable or of the becoming.

Undoubtedly, Western thought believes that determinacy as such (beings *qua* beings ['l'ente in quanto ente', t/n], the positive *qua* positive) is becoming. But this belief belongs to the essence of the faith in becoming, i.e. it belongs to the essence of nihilism. On the contrary, outside of nihilism, the originary structure of truth, as the originary unity of the opposition between positive and negative and of the appearing of the positive, is the appearing of the necessity that determinacy *as such* is eternal (because to affirm that beings, the positive, become – that it comes out of nothing and returns to it – is to affirm that beings are nothing, that the positive is negative); so that the originary structure of truth is simultaneously the originary unity of the appearing of the eternity of determinacy as such, and of the appearing of the self-negation of the negation of determinacy.

One more observation. The Aristotelian *élenchos* should not be confused with another great theme, almost ignored but also present in the fourth book of Aristotle's *Metaphysics*: the impossibility that consciousness be convinced of contradiction (cf. *The Essence of Nihilism*, cit., 'Aletheia', pp. 415 et seq.). In other words, it is one thing to show that the negation of determinacy necessarily presupposes determinacy; it is another thing to show that it is impossible for consciousness to be convinced of the negation of determinacy (i.e. that not only the content of the error, but the error itself, cannot exist) – even though the two themes are essentially connected, for showing that the negation of determinacy presupposes determinacy means showing that pure error does not exist, but emerges within truth.

But before delving into these rarely explored themes – in which it appears that the principle of non-contradiction not only excludes the *contradictoriness* of beings but *also* the *self-contradicting* of consciousness itself – today's philosophical reflection on the meaning of the *Book IV* of the *Metaphysics* must first be reminded of the distinction between contradicting oneself and contradictoriness (this is the theme touched upon in the pages of this book in Chapter 6, sections 4–5); and *at this first level* of reflection on the principle of non-contradiction (a level, moreover, that a certain part of contemporary thought seems unable to rise to), one must say that this principle does *not* affirm the impossibility of the self-contradicting of thinking, but the impossibility of the contradictoriness of beings (and certainly also of that being which is thinking, in the sense that it is not other than itself).

The inability to rise to this distinction has produced the criticisms that analytic thought has addressed to the Marxian concept of contradiction (cf. here, Chapter 6, sections 4–5). Yet, once this distinction has been brought to light, one must realize that the impossibility of negating the opposition of the positive and the negative is simultaneously (as Aristotle shows in the *Book IV* of the *Metaphysics*) the impossibility that the appearing of the positive is the conviction that the positive is the negative.[9]

5

What is Europe?

1

Nowadays, this question has a myriad of answers: as many as there are types of knowledge within which the problem of the meaning of what we call 'Europe' is posited. Nowadays, the multiplication of answers concerns not only Europe but every possible object of which one wants to know the identity. Today, the dominant form of knowledge is scientific knowledge, that is, the set of cognitive attitudes that emerge precisely because they rigorously *isolate* specific fields of research. These attitudes make it fundamentally impossible to have any knowledge that aims to grasp the unified meaning of isolated, specific fields of research, and thus of the object that in each of these fields ends up presenting a different aspect. Europe is studied in terms of geographical and natural sciences, historical and social sciences, ethnology and anthropology, economics and political sciences, philosophical and linguistic sciences. In each of these research fields, one believes one can establish what Europe is: the result is that what is presented is not Europe, but many Europes, as many as there are scientific specializations concerned with the phenomenon of 'Europe', and whose coming together in a unified meaning can only be a more or less accidental juxtaposition.

On the other hand, the successes of modern science are due to its specialization and its isolating attitude. Isolation is the fundamental condition of action: one acts only insofar as one believes one can control a specific field of objects, that is, only insofar as one believes the field can be isolated from the context in which it is found. Therefore, the specialized character of science, according to which science coincides with rationality *tout court*, is the application to the cognitive plane of the fundamental condition of action: the faith that reality is a multiplicity of parts originarily separate from one another and unified in accidental and ultimately arbitrary syntheses. The growth of power is proportional to the intensity of such faith. This finds its ultimate celebration in the civilization of technics, that is, in the civilization that arranges the greatest capacity for domination ever seen on Earth: the scientific–technological Apparatus.

2

Precisely because the isolating attitude of science reproduces the isolation that makes action possible, isolation reaches its peak in the civilization of technics and science. Yet, it does not originate with it.

However, one should observe that in the civilization of technics, Europe is not only subjected to the cognitive fragmentation imposed by modern science, but also to the political–economic fragmentation due to the current international situation. Indeed, there are great forces pushing for the economic–political unification of Europe, but even greater forces are obstructing its realization.

Firstly, just as the attempt to unify the isolated fields of scientific research is a juxtaposition of parts that cannot overcome their originary isolation, so the political unification of Europe – and, in general, any action aimed at unifying a plurality of goals – is inevitably a juxtaposition of goals. This is a structural dysfunction, originating from the impossibility of unifying goals (and means) that are conceived as originarily separate in their essence. Precisely because action is isolation, the aggregation of different actions and goals is accidental and precarious and is fundamentally exposed to the possibility of disintegration.

Undoubtedly, the advanced forms of European capitalism aim for the unification of the democracies of Western Europe, because the logic of capitalism still requires the elimination of national constraints and the expansion of the market. The political fragmentation of Europe prevents the freedom of movement of capital, yet this is needed to compete with North American and Japanese markets. Additionally, political unity in Europe could ease the still unresolved issue of the possible strengthening of communist parties in Western Europe. If in the Italian Parliament the growth of the PCI ['Italian Communist Party', t/n] or, more generally, of left-wing forces would create issues difficult to solve, the European Parliament, with its large centre-right majority, could, for a long time, absorb, without trauma, the sectoral growth of the left.

But the forces tending to hinder the political unification of Europe are far more substantial (and the example given above of the factors of unification is far from being complete). In effect, one tends to forget that the unification of Europe would equate to the birth of a third global superpower, which would bring about a gigantic shift in the balance of power and could not fail to concern those who currently guide the fate of the world, that is, the USA–USSR Duumvirate. After all, this is why forty years after the Second World War, the third and final world war has not yet broken out. In effect, as a third superpower, Europe complicates the global game. In a parliament, the bipolarism of balancing forces is paralyzing, but on the world stage, the overcoming of balance and paralysis is an unknown ['un'incognita', t/n] far more threatening than the inconvenience it aims to remedy. Political unification would lead to a tremendous economic (and thus military) strengthening of Europe, and if such unification happened within the context of the North Atlantic Pact, the Soviet Union would be forced to further increase its economic productivity and its ability to convert this into military economy.

For the USSR, the unity of Europe is a major danger to be avoided. But it is also a danger for the United States, for whom a militarily stronger Europe is certainly advantageous, yet politically and economically subordinated. That is, incapable of becoming, like the USA, a peer of the Soviet Union. In the capitalist world, the growing internal conflict and competition, due to the rise of integrated European capitalism, could weaken the defences against the pressure from communist countries. Therefore, as it presents itself nowadays, the unification of Europe is highly destabilizing and contains serious dangers for world peace.

3

Luigi Einaudi used to speak of the 'ancient and universal experience' ['esperienza antichissima e universale', t/n] that teaches how the 'force' ['forza', t/n] of the state curbs internal anarchy. Similarly, Einaudi used to argue that only 'force' ['forza', t/n] could be the remedy against the anarchy existing between European peoples – the force constituted by a 'Super-State' ['super–Stato', t/n] capable of controlling and punishing the states that seek to perpetuate 'massacre and wholesale robbery' ['le carneficine e i latrocinî all'ingrosso', t/n]. For Einaudi, the United States of Europe would in fact be the 'superstate' capable of preventing a new war between European countries.

Today, it is well known that the threat of war does not come from conflict between European states, but from the tension between the USA and the USSR. Nonetheless, it is much less known that such planetary tension is linked to the actual capacity of the two superpowers to create the first real, non-utopian form of the Super-State that Einaudi spoke of. Namely, the 'force' capable of carrying out those global police functions that allow for the safeguarding of peace. The conceptual model that Einaudi relied on is the political philosophy of Hobbes. Even Max Weber's definition of the state as the 'legitimate monopoly of force' can be traced back to Hobbes. On a planetary level, it is precisely the USA–USSR Duumvirate that should be looked at as the 'State' *par excellence*, as the Super-State.

Indeed, if the legitimate monopoly of force requires the subjects' faith in the legitimacy of the monopoly, this faith does not require unanimity, but the existence of a dominant tendency. This means that just as the traditional state is the legitimate monopoly of force even when there are forces (non-dominant) within it that seek to overthrow that monopoly, so the duumviral Super-State is the legitimate monopoly of force until the Third World, China, Japan and Europe succeed in destroying the duumviral monopoly. Furthermore, in the subjects' faith in the legitimacy of the monopoly of force, the meaning of 'legitimacy' is extremely vague (exactly because this is no scientific definition of legitimacy, but the meaning of legitimacy as seen through the eyes of the subjects, so that the faith in the legitimacy of the monopoly of force ultimately boils down to the acceptance of the monopoly, that is, to the absence of rebellion capable of eliminating it). Precisely for this reason, the duumviral monopoly is legitimate as long as it manages to curb the pressure from below that seeks to eliminate it. All this means that the duumviral monopoly tends to prevent anything that, like the political unification of Europe, would put it at risk.

Undoubtedly, reality is more imperfect than the utopia and the duumviral Super-State may degenerate into a direct confrontation between its two members – just as, in the traditional form of the state, conflicts can arise between different forms of power and between different social groups. But despite the anomaly and the danger of its form, the duumviral Super-State manages to realize the first actual form of a world 'federation', where the unifying element is certainly not a consensus expressed in a unified legislative body, but the *duumviri*'s awareness that they are the forces upon whose relationship the destiny of the world depends.

4

Thus, Europe reveals itself as a multiplicity of isolated Europes within the various forms of scientific specialization (i.e. the form of knowledge that is currently dominant on Earth); and, at the same time, Europe (that is, what 'Europe' is from the standpoint of scientific specialization) is subjected to the action of the global Duumvirate, which seeks to perpetuate the existing separation between the various parts and aspects of European reality. If on one hand, in the isolating attitude of science the isolation in which action is grounded is repeated ['si ripropone', t/n], on the other hand, the action that nowadays has the greatest power on Earth isolates its field of application following the criteria of scientific isolation. The duumviral action (and certainly not only the duumviral action) aims for the maximum of power, freeing itself from any ideological configuration, in order to be predominantly guided (and, to the limit, exclusively guided) by the rationality of scientific planning. The duumviral Super-State (that is, the contradiction it embodies as the unity of opposing goals – see Chapter 2, 4) is the dominant form of the scientific–technological Apparatus.

Even the type of unification represented by the duumviral Super-State is an accidental and precarious juxtaposition of the isolated and divergent purposes of the two superpowers, but this unification has an extremely greater strength than all the unifications that aim to oppose it, and the resulting combination of its divergent goals has the capacity to control and determine every other resultant.

The complex system of fragmentation and shattering – first of all carried out by scientific culture and the type of action practiced by the duumviral Super-State – prevents any talk of a unified meaning or reality of Europe.

If the meaning of reality is the one offered by science, then in the confrontation between accidental aggregates (unifications), the stronger aggregates prevail, and just as the duumviral aggregate is able to impose itself, on a planetary level, over all other forms of aggregation, so in the clash between the various meanings which Europe presents in scientific specialization, the strongest meaning ends up prevailing, that is, that of economic Europe: Europe as seen from the perspective of political economy, i.e. Europe as the organization of the scientific–technological Apparatus. And the most consistent drive toward political unification of Europe is given by the European needs of organizing that Apparatus. In such a context, the other meanings and purposes of European reality are subordinated to the economic–technological purpose, even though – until this subordination is fully realized – there is also a form of political eclecticism, so widespread in Western democracies, which declares its intent to uphold, around the core of the economic–technological Apparatus, the so-called 'values' of European civilization.

5

The logic of action, the logic of science and the logic of the duumviral Super-State are all, albeit in a specific manner, logics of isolation. The logic of isolation (which Hegel used to call the 'logic of the intellect') is characteristic of the contemporary world; yet its roots lie deep in the origins of our civilization, namely, in Ancient Greek thought. First and foremost, this means that with Ancient Greek thought begins to appear the meaning of action which has imposed itself over ever larger areas of the Western European regions.

Even before the Ancient Greeks, humans act, and even pre-Ancient Greek action is isolation.[1] But in Ancient Greek thought, action acquires an extreme radicality. On one hand, this radicality is due to the radical nature of isolation, and on the other hand, it is due to the conviction that this radical meaning of action is the content of an incontrovertible knowledge, namely, philosophy, understood as *epistéme*.

Plato defines action as 'production' and defines production as any 'cause' that brings things 'from nothingness into being', so that every action performed in every 'technics' makes someone a producer (*Convivium*, 205 b–c).[2] Our culture still struggles to grasp the profound nature of the Ancient Greek reflection on the infinite opposition between being and the absolute negativity of nothingness; however, the unprecedented nature of this opposition determines the radical nature of the action which the Ancient Greeks begin to conceive and according to which they begin to exist. Before the Ancient Greeks, humans did not bring things from nothingness to being because 'nothingness' and 'being' did not yet indicate the terms of an infinite opposition. In this opposition, nothingness is no longer the not being this or that aspect of the world, this or that dimension of the universe, but it is the not being any aspect, any dimension, that is, it is the not being anything, any *'thing'* ['alcun"ché"', t/n]. Every 'thing' contributes to forming the whole, the totality of being, beyond which there is only nothingness, that is, there is nothing ['non c'è che il niente, ossia non c'è niente', t/n], there is no 'thing'. Thus, for the Ancient Greeks, birth and death start to mean coming out of nothingness and returning to it. The Ancient Greeks and the world itself, as viewed by the Ancient Greeks, begin to be born and to die in an unprecedented way. Divine and human demiurges are the producers that determine the birth and death of natural and artificial beings. Plato's 'Republic' itself is the human organization of production: it is not the utopia of a philosopher, but the demiurgic dimension in which all the great phenomena of what we call 'European history' have manifested themselves and in which they have taken meaning, up to the transfer of the monopoly of world dominance from Europe to the United States and the Soviet Union.

The Ancient Greek meaning of action includes the belief that the becoming of the world is a coming out of nothingness and a going to nothingness on the part of things, their 'oscillation' (*epamphoterízein*, says Plato in the *Republic*, 479 c) between being and nothingness. This very belief is the true and crucial demarcation in the history of humankind, something radically more essential than any sociological, ethnological or religious connotation, such as those that identify the decisive turn in history with the appearance of a 'saviour' or in the transition from matriarchy to patriarchy. This belief is more decisive, because the Ancient Greek meaning of being and nothingness, and therefore of becoming and acting, has the capacity to envelop every other meaning and to give a new weight and imprint to the very concepts of 'salvation', 'patriarchy', 'matriarchy', and to every other concept. When placed in relation to the unprecedented meaning of being and nothingness, of becoming and acting, all things and all meanings acquire an unprecedented meaning, and the entire face of the world undergoes a transformation that pulls it decisively away from its previous form.

The Ancient Greek meaning of becoming is the foundation, the anticipation, and the essential dimension of the isolation that lies at the foundation of modern science and of the planetary power relations, where the duumviral domination of the Earth is the highest form so far achieved of isolation produced by scientific–technological action. Indeed, that which comes out of nothingness cannot have forerunners ['dei battistrada'] which, for it ['per lui', t/n], have already built bridges to the already-existent ['il già esistente', t/n], thereby linking the existent to the non-existent. What comes out of nothing, precisely because it is such, cannot have any connection with the existent: when it emerges, it has not made any previous pact with the existent, it cannot have any relationship with it, it cannot have any purpose. Therefore, it arrives as something simply and absolutely juxtaposed to the already-existent, entirely accidental with respect to it, and therefore absolutely *isolated* from the context in which it finds itself. Starting from the Ancient Greeks – stretching from the subterranean layers of their thought to the explicitness of contemporary culture – the already-existent, precisely because it is traversed and immersed in the unprecedented meaning of becoming, emerges as an accidental aggregate of things. Thus, the world becomes this aggregate, precisely because one remains within the belief that things have come out of nothingness and are inclined to return to nothingness once again. The Ancient Greeks invent the extreme and unprecedented meaning of becoming (that is, of time, history, action, production, creation, destruction). With this invention, they bring to light the *isolation* of things that finds its concrete expression in what we call 'European history' and culminates in the civilization of technics. And, for now, in the duumviral administration of the planet.

6

The will to isolate things begins *in the underground*, in the unexpressed, implicit dimension of Ancient Greek thought, and remains long hidden in the underground of European culture and society. That happens because, on the other hand, the *explicit* will of Ancient Greek thought is *to unify* the multiplicity of the world. Once again, it is a matter of understanding that this will to unify is doomed to failure because it is itself grounded in the Ancient Greek faith in becoming, and because this faith is the very principle of the extreme form of isolation.

In Ancient Greek philosophy – and throughout the history of *epistéme* – the will to unify is the will to understand *the* world's unified and definitive Meaning ['Senso', t/n]. The will to unify the multiplicity that oscillates between being and nothingness is at the heart ['è l'anima', t/n] of all the major events in European tradition, from the Roman Empire to the universal Church, from the 'catholicity' of Christianity to the unification of the world by capitalism, and to the unification of workers by Marxism. Each of these unifications presents itself as the definitive and immutable Meaning of reality and history, but such a Meaning aims to unify what is originarily assumed to be an oscillation between being and nothingness, thus non-unifiable, as a multiplicity essentially unrelated to itself, which, sooner or later, reveals the illusion of every synthesis that seeks to bestow a definitive unity to the multiplicity ['molteplice', t/n].

The 'liberation' of the modern human being is, precisely, liberation from any definitive and immutable unification of the becoming multiplicity ['il molteplice diveniente', t/n] – first and foremost, from the becoming of humanity ['divenire umano', t/n]. In essence, contemporary culture's denial of the existence of an *epistéme*, that is, of an incontrovertible truth that shows the definitive Meaning of the world is the denial of the possibility of a definitive synthesis – that is, a 'synthesis a priori' – that could unify the isolated parts of the world. Coming out of nothingness and aggregating themselves to what is temporarily in being, these parts are isolated from one another: They cannot entertain relationships that are not contingent, provisional, non-necessary, accidental.

This is true even though contemporary culture continues to ignore the authentic meaning of its fundamental dependence on Ancient Greek thought, and therefore continues to ignore the fact that scientific specialization and the radicality of action, and thus the isolation produced by the civilization of technics, are the truest expression and the inevitable consequence of the Ancient Greek meaning of action, becoming, being and nothingness.

Certainly, one acknowledges that if there is no definitive truth, then there can be no centre to reality and knowledge, so that both dissolve into a plurality of isolated and unrelated parts. However, one is not able to understand that the authentic reason for the denial of any definitive truth is the will to isolate, the kind of separating will belonging to the essence of the Ancient Greek faith in the oscillation of things between being and nothingness. In this context, one can see the fundamental reason for the fated failure of Hegelian (and Marxist) dialectics in its attempt to transcend the separating will (the 'intellect') by relying on the faith in becoming.

Thus, in Western thought, the unification (*a priori* synthesis) of the becoming multiplicity – which is simultaneously the affirmation of the definitive, immutable Meaning of that multiplicity – is doomed to failure because, on one hand, it is the entification of nothingness, from which the determinations of multiplicity come into being (cf. Chapter 2, sections 9–10), and on the other hand, the unification fails because the determinations of the multiplicity, as they oscillate between being and nothingness, are originarily isolated from each other, so that any unification of them can only be accidental and casual.

7

Hence, scientific specialization does not enable us to know what Europe is and presents a multiplicity of isolated Europes; the peak of dominance reached by the duumviral Super-State is the peak of the isolating action. And with respect to 'Europe', such peak hinders the attempts at an economic–political unification of European nations. *Yet*, the isolating will, which belongs to the essence of the Ancient Greek faith in becoming, is the very opening of the unified dimension in which all the major events forming European history unfold and find meaning. Europe is the specific will for separation and division that appears with the Ancient Greek reflection on the meaning of being, nothingness and becoming.

Therefore, it is not a coincidence that no other civilization knows the volume of struggles and contradictions present in European history. The same planetary clash currently taking place between the two superpowers is the continuation of the traditional way in which hegemonic European states have dominated the world in antagonism with each other, thus imperfectly realizing that planetary order which the duumviral Super-State is now realizing with incomparably greater effectiveness. In fact, the relationship between isolated parts can only be conflictual: their unification is always a mask for conflict. In its extreme form, conflict belongs to the soul of Europe. It is no coincidence that the root of the two World Wars is European and that the possibility of a conflict capable of annihilating humanity is due to the specifically European factor represented by technics.

This is not to say that conflict is absent from non-European civilizations. Even in these civilizations, actions take place, and thus isolation takes place. Nevertheless, in those civilizations, the Ancient Greek meaning of action remains still unexpressed, implicit, and this enables European action to take place as an isolation much more radical than all the forms of action and isolation that appear in non-European civilizations. The East is not the liberation from the disease of isolation and conflict: the East is the incubation state of the disease. But if in 'our' culture every definitive truth has faded, the idea that conflict is a 'disease' cannot be a definitive truth; on the contrary, this represents the mere expression of a repulsion for conflict, which is spreading among the privileged peoples of the planet. A repulsion that is precarious and unreliable, for it is itself experienced within the isolating faith in the Ancient Greek meaning of becoming, which is the very foundation of conflict.

But the faith in the origination of things from nothingness and in their return to it is the foundation of conflict – and therefore of the violence of the domination – not only because the relationship between the isolated parts of the world is unavoidably conflictual (in effect, for what is isolated, the relationship with the other is something essentially foreign and thus inassimilable and violent), but also because – as already mentioned – the extreme form of the will to power is only possible if one believes that things are detached from being and therefore can be seized, modified, controlled, produced, destroyed. The faith in the existence of becoming is the foundation of the will to power of the West.

At this point, one cannot reply by saying that if one had no faith in the existence *of things*, no plan of domination could arise (and that, therefore, this further type of faith serves as the foundation of the will to power). One cannot reply in this way because if one thinks that all things are eternal, immutable and therefore unmodifiable, no plan of domination can arise; hence, such a project does not emerge in relation to the faith in the existence of things (or beings, or being) *as such*, but in relation to the faith in the existence of things *as becoming*. The plan of domination reaches its peak when the becoming of things (and therefore action) is understood according to the meaning given to it by Ancient Greek thought.

The extreme form of the culmination of the plan of domination is the twilight of the immutable in the civilization of technics. Nowadays, this presents itself as the arrangement of the scientific–technological Apparatus operated by the duumviral Super-State. Therefore, one cannot believe, as for example happens with Heidegger, that Europe is an alternative to the Soviet and American worlds. Of course, the European lifestyle and culture still present features that are gradually disappearing in the USA and the USSR. But in its essence, Europe is the dimension from which the domination over the 'ideologies' that the scientific–technological Apparatus has taken on in the USA and the USSR legitimately develops.

Moreover, it is well known that even the features of European life (where the Apparatus is more subjected to the criticisms of the Western tradition) are disappearing. American society remains the model to which European society, and to a different extent, other societies of the planet (including Russian society) are progressively approaching. Particularly in the USA, the capitalist logic, which governs the economic arrangement of the scientific–technological Apparatus, is more consistent with the logic of the Apparatus than the Marxist logic, by which this arrangement is guided in the USSR. Indeed, capitalism explicitly takes place within the logic of isolation, while Marxism expressly presents itself as the negation of this (although this negation, as an *a priori* epistemic ['epistemica', t/n] synthesis, is destined to fail). This is not to say that capitalism is not an 'ideology' and can be assimilated without residues into scientific rationality: it is to say that in capitalism, the logic of production and distribution aims to reduce such residues. That is, it aims to be consistent, unlike the explicit intentions of Marxist economics, with a conception of the world as an accidental aggregate of isolated parts and therefore (this time, along with certain forms of Marxist culture) with scientific rationality. This conception is also attributable to Marxism (and for this reason, attempts to show the solidarity between Marxism and scientific rationality can make sense): but *despite* its intentions. On the other hand, there is no need to remove the explicit intentions of capitalist culture to show its alignment with the logic of isolation.

Europe is not an alternative to the American and Soviet worlds. Yet the question: 'What is Europe?' cannot receive an answer until the Ancient Greek faith in the existence of becoming is questioned. Europe 'grows' within this faith, in the sense that this faith is the backdrop of all the events forming European civilization and of the entire West. But this definition still leaves aside the most decisive issue: the one that does not consider the faith in becoming as something evident, indeed as the supreme self-evidence – as happens throughout the entire history of the West – but as something that must answer for its unconditional dominance.

8

What is called 'the West' – in its relationship with all other forms of civilization – appears in interpreting ['nell'interpretare', t/n] (cf. *Destino della Necessità*, op. cit., Chapter XV). In other words, it appears because the interpreting *wants*, following certain rules, what appears to have a determinate meaning. The interpretive will has no incontrovertible foundation: it is not the self-imposition or *standing* of the meaning ['lo stare del senso', t/n], but, precisely, the will for meaning. The interpretive will belongs to the essence of the will to power.

Yet once they are willed, the rules of the interpreting entail certain consequences (among these rules, there are also the rules that establish the methods of drawing the consequences according to the adopted rules). In fact, it is precisely according to these rules that it is here stated that Europe and the West grow within the faith in becoming, that is, that this faith is the determination present in every form of Western civilization, the identical element within the diversity of the forms of the West, the unity of the multiplicity of those forms. (And precisely because this faith is the identity present in the different forms, it is said in my writings that the faith in becoming is the 'dimension', the 'ground', the 'area' ['ambito', t/n], the 'space', the 'place' in which the forms of the West 'grow'.)

The scientific–technological Apparatus is the most rigorous and powerful form of the faith in becoming (even though this faith is currently among the least aware of its ontological character), and is, in turn, the unification of a multiplicity of forms of Western civilization. However, the unification here has a different meaning: the Apparatus is not, unlike the faith in becoming, an identical content that makes itself known, visible in the different forms (Christianity, philosophy, Church, State, capitalism, science, Marxism, technics, etc.), but it is the ability to subordinate to its own purpose (the unlimited increase of power) the purposes of the different forms.

Even the faith in becoming is a will (that subordinates to itself the pre-ontological forms of the will ['del volere', t/n]), but it does not recognize ['conosce', t/n] itself as will, that is, it does not recognize itself as will and as faith. On the other hand, the Apparatus is a will that already recognizes itself as will (even though it does not recognize the faith of becoming as will and as faith). For this reason, the faith in becoming subordinates to itself the forms of the West, in the sense that it is present in each of them, it is the essence of each one; whereas the Apparatus (i.e. the most powerful form assumed by the faith in becoming) subordinates all the forms of the West, in the sense that it has the power to make its purpose prevail over theirs.

The faith in becoming cannot recognize itself as faith (on the contrary, it recognizes itself as supreme self-evidence), yet it can recognize itself as the unity of the cultural multiplicity ['molteplice culturale', t/n] formed by the different forms of the West. All those attitudes in contemporary culture (which are themselves forms of the faith in becoming), which exclude any identity of (in) the differences and do not realize that the unity of the West consists in affirming the existence of becoming, are inadequate to the possibilities of self-consciousness of this faith. Such affirmation inevitably leads to the affirmation of the isolation of the determinations of the becoming multiplicity; but the isolating attitude is precisely the trait present (implicitly or explicitly) in all forms of the West, and thus it is the trait that unifies the multiplicity of forms.

The faith in becoming can also come to realize that the scientific-technological Apparatus is the most rigorous form it can assume, the one in which the totality ['l'insieme', t/n] of the immutable is 'destined' to decline. (Undoubtedly, this 'destination' cannot appear to this faith according to the meaning of *destiny*, which has always and forever opened outside it; but it can appear according to the meaning where 'destination' is – cf. above, Chapter 3, sections 9–10 – the appearing of the contradiction of the entification of nothing.) In other words, the faith in becoming can come to realize that the Apparatus is the unification of the forms of the West, because it has the power to subordinate to its purpose their own purposes.

Like all typical forms of contemporary culture, in relation to its field, neofunctionalist sociology (for example, N. Luhmann) denies that society forms a unity or describable totality ['globalità descrivibile', t/n]. According to neofunctionalist sociology, a society consists of partial systems (politics, economy, law, public health, education, religion) and these have the task of solving certain issues and cannot be permanently ordered in a certain hierarchy: Each of which gives primacy to its own function, regarding the other systems as its environment. This means that there is a conflict between social systems, which is temporarily resolved in favour of the systems that are technically fiercer.

But if, instead of considering society *in general*, one considers the way people associate nowadays on Earth, one cannot avoid acknowledging that the entire planet has taken the form of a unified society, because a hierarchy actually exists on Earth: the one where the capitalist–socialist administration of the Apparatus subordinates all the partial systems to itself, and where the states themselves become partial systems of the Apparatus. If neofunctionalism acknowledges the conflict between systems, which always establishes a hierarchy between the dominant and the subordinate systems, then it cannot fail to acknowledge that conflict and, therefore, the dominant hierarchy where the Apparatus is the super-system that subordinates all other systems to itself. The unity of the planetary society *is* describable following the same interpretive rules that lead to the acknowledgement of conflict between different social systems.

In an analogous fashion, when one asks whether the 'driving force' of economic development is represented by the 'large apparatuses' (understood as 'military, financial, telematic, technical–scientific groups'), *or* by businesses, one does not realize that, apart from the fact that businesses themselves already form an 'apparatus' (in the reduced sense attributed to the term in that context), the logic of the alternative – enterprises or 'apparatuses' – is inadequate, for it refers to a level subordinate to the primary one of the Apparatus as a unified structure of the large apparatuses. The true 'growth engine' ['motore dello sviluppo', t/n] is the will of the Apparatus to reproduce itself and to increase its power without limit. Thus, the *concordia discors* of the USA–USSR (i.e. the two primary incarnations of the Apparatus) represents the driving planetary entrepreneurship.

Therefore, there is no scenario in which sequences from scientific inventions to the economy, from the economy to inventions, and from military needs to inventions and economy *are aligned*: These sequences do not align, but are arranged in a hierarchical order where the Demand of the Apparatus activates ['mobilita'] inventions, the economy and military needs – since, as for the latter, the will of the Apparatus to endlessly increase its power is also the will to destroy everything that threatens growth. It is true that the current dominance of the Apparatus is not guaranteed forever and that no hierarchy among the 'systems' is final, but at the moment, there are no forces in sight capable of subordinating the Apparatus' purpose to their own. That is not all. Indeed, if such forces were to appear, they would be the most powerful forms of the will to power and, therefore, they would be the true Apparatus. Therefore, the current dominance of the scientific–technological Apparatus is not guaranteed forever, in the sense that the current configuration of the Apparatus is not guaranteed to remain dominant.

By denying any 'unity of difference' and any 'unity in reality' on the grounds of the concept of 'functional differentiation', even neofunctionalism affirms the mutual *isolation* of social systems and of their elements. Yet, neofunctionalism does not possess a logic that allows it to firmly hold what it implicitly affirms, that is, that social isolation (and theoretical isolation), be this implicit or explicit, is the unifying element of European history. Moreover, the criticism that sociological neofunctionalism directs at *ontology* considers an aspect of ontology that, although emerging in the history of European culture, is still a limited aspect: the *traditional* aspect of ontology, where ontology ties the determinations of the world to their stable foundation, to the immutable hierarchy, to the final centre and peak. Nevertheless, it is in fact ontology understood as the evocation of the immutables. And this ontology is destined to be destroyed not by a non-ontological attitude, but by the rigorization of ontology itself, which, freeing the becoming of beings from the immutables, affirms the reciprocal indifference of beings, that is, their isolation. The logic of isolation is the most rigorous form of Ancient Greek ontology.

9

The West does not only appear to itself (and, in general, within non-truth ['non-verità', t/n]): The West also appears (in its relationship with other forms of civilization) in the gaze of truth, which since ever and forever remains outside any will of isolation. Outside the isolating will, truth is *destiny*. This word (cf. *Destino della Necessità, op. cit.*) indicates the authentic standing that *epistéme* has vainly tried to be.

In the destiny (i.e. in the standing) of truth, the West reveals itself, in the sense that the very interpretation on which the West is grounded reveals itself. Yet, in the destiny of truth, the 'identity' of the different forms of Western civilization (that is, the faith in becoming) and the 'destination' of the West to the civilization of technics do not simply appear according to the character and strength that such 'identity' and such 'destination' present in the possible self-consciousness of the West (this self-consciousness – which is 'possible' because the West has not yet achieved it, even though it could, in principle – is in fact brought to light above in Chapter 3). In the destiny of truth, 'identity', 'difference' and 'destination' acquire a fundamentally different meaning, which is due to their belonging to the unchanging and incontrovertible standing of the destiny of truth.

And the very 'standing' of the destiny of truth is essentially different from the 'standing' of *epistéme*. The faith in becoming makes any standing impossible – and thus every immutable, every centre, every final unity of the multiplicity. However, in the destiny of truth, this faith appears as the extreme alienation and therefore, the destruction of epistemic standing appears to be an event internal to alienation. In the destiny of truth, standing has an essentially different meaning, because it is no longer the will to dominate becoming.

Therefore, the language alluding to the authentic standing of the destiny can finally speak of the 'unchanging and incontrovertible standing', which cannot be shaken or made to waver by anything. That language can speak of the 'unity', the 'centre' of the multiplicity, the 'eternal truth', the 'eternity of every being', without these determinations being swamped by the process of the destruction of the immutables belonging to *epistéme* and the tradition of the West. Therefore, that language can also speak – in a profoundly different sense from the one present in the self-consciousness of the West – of the unifying element of Europe and the West: the faith in becoming, in which the will of isolation is grounded that rules out any unifying principle of the becoming multiplicity.

6

Notes on the Italian state of affairs

1

There can be no 'peace and security' in our country if it does not manage to stay close to the centre of the capitalist system. The more Italy moves toward the periphery – this also applies to other Western democracies – the more it is subjected to a dual pressure: the pressure of the system, which intends to keep our country within its orbit and prevent its possible defection from strengthening the opposing system, and the pressure of the opposing system – real socialism – which seeks to favour (directly or indirectly) the defection. Internal peace and security decrease in proportion to the growing intensity of these two conflicting pressures. It is no coincidence that in the centres of both systems – the USA and the USSR – political terrorism and uprisings against the state apparatus are essentially absent.

On the other hand, Italy can remain close to the centre only if its productive apparatus is of a piece with the apparatus of the system. Yet this means that Italian industry is forced to take the path of factory automation, along which other capitalist countries have already been marching for some time. Except that increased automation means increased unemployment. In turn, mass unemployment would push the electorate to the left and produce a decisive advance of the Italian Communist Party (PCI): in the sense that, given today's configuration of the PCI, such a decisive advance would be intolerable for the security of the system. It would be a change that would push Italy to the periphery of the system where there can be no peace and security for our society.

Thus, one finds oneself in a strongly *paradoxical* situation (which has a structure quite similar to that of so-called 'logical' or 'syntactic' paradoxes): to stay close to the centre of the system, our country must innovate its productive apparatus. Yet the political–social consequences of this apparatus push it away from that centre; or, in other words: the economic conditions required for peace and security in Italy determine a situation in which the peace and security of Italian society are put at risk.

On one hand, the crucial factor leading to innovation and automation in the productive apparatus is given by the tension between the capitalist and communist blocs, and on the other hand, it is given by the tension where the two blocs are united and opposed to the poor countries of the Third World. The struggle between capitalism and real socialism is a fight between the rich who compete for world domination. In this planetary perspective, the world proletariat no longer includes the working class of the Northern countries, be this capitalist or communist.

The struggle between the rich for world domination and the fight that the rich wage to prevent the poor from threatening their supremacy and privileges drive the rich countries to an unprecedented degree of productive activity. In USA–USSR relations, this aims to continuously balance out the technological–military advantages achieved by the adversary, whereas in the rich–poor relationship, it seeks to preserve the advantage that the productive apparatus of the rich has over that of the poor. (This is in no way in contradiction with the programs of aid to the Third World: indeed, these imply that the aid will not reach the point where it could enable the Third World to threaten the existing privileged situation.) Such a dual intent requires that the rich countries push the process of innovation and automation of their productive apparatus to the fullest. Yet in its concrete configuration, the productive apparatus is the scientific–technological Apparatus. But in turn, this aims to become ever more powerful, independently of the goals that the world powers intend to achieve through its control and usage. The Apparatus prevents these forces from remaining mere utopias, while the will to power within them fuels the will of the Apparatus to indefinitely increase its power. Now, all of this requires a constant renewal of products and means of production.

Thus, the configuration of global relations produces a scenario that leads to the opposite of economic stagnation. Precisely because of the conflicting nature of their relations and of the relationship they entertain with the rest of the world, the two superpowers have become – as we have already noted – the two largest planetary entrepreneurs, who ensure technological innovation and economic growth. Even the two empires of which these superpowers are the centre foster this economic dynamism, for they are committed to keeping pace with the leaders or not falling too far behind.

As a planetary entrepreneur, the duumviral superstate of the USA–USSR gives new energy to the traditional forms of capital, albeit placing them in a subordinate position – those are the forms that nowadays in Italy urgently demand the automation of the industrial apparatus, i.e. the transformation that produces the *paradox* mentioned earlier.

Yet, it is still the international situation that suggests the way out of the paradox. Technics (the scientific–technological Apparatus) has the potential to 'solve the main problems' of humanity on Earth. Nevertheless, before this theoretical possibility becomes a real fact, an intermediate phase must take place, during which the poor countries, still experiencing high population growth, will seek to improve their situation in the world by taking wealth from where it currently resides. This will be one of the most difficult moments for the privileged peoples. But it is precisely the approach of this greater danger that will make the 'paradoxical situation', which our country is heading toward, seem insignificant by comparison.

Today, one struggles to resolve the issue of the link between automation and unemployment, but solutions will emerge forcefully when one realizes that the struggle between workers and capital in rich countries will have to be addressed in order to confront the increasingly violent pressure of the international proletariat on the rich countries, including Italy. Those who think that if industrial transformation in Italy grows the left, such an inconvenience could be eliminated by a right-wing authoritarian turn, would be mistaken ('mistaken', from the perspective of the interests of the rich). Indeed, with the blow of the world proletariat, right-wing authoritarian regimes would be the first to succumb, forced to defend themselves both on the external and internal fronts. Therefore, it is not 'prudent' (again, from the perspective of the interests of the rich) to waste energy and foster resentment in the tug-of-war between masters and workers. A secondary clash ['uno scontro di retroguardia', t/n].

2

In Italy, the 'destabilizing' factor is not terrorism: it is the Italian Communist Party (PCI). In its relevant meaning, such a seemingly paradoxical statement is substantially shared by the PCI itself: precisely because this still explicitly aims to change the current economic–political balance of Italian society and thus to reform the network of relationships that the governing political class maintains with its Western allies. If one refers to the stability of this balance and this network, the PCI is and wants to be 'destabilizing'. On the other hand, though, if one refers to the stability of parliamentary democracy, the PCI nowadays does not intend to threaten it. On the contrary, in today's political situation, the PCI is the party that has the greatest interest in appearing and being democratic – and in this sense, the PCI is a stabilizing factor for the amount of democracy that currently exists in Italy. Exactly because it fears a shift to the right in Italian society, the PCI has every interest in embodying the codes of parliamentary democracy and the forms of the republican Constitution as much as possible: so that it becomes as clear as possible that an anti-communist shift to the right would be (precisely because it is anti-communist) anti-democratic and unconstitutional.

Nonetheless, it is undisputable that, in the Western sphere, the PCI (even the one advocating the 'third way') suggests a kind of socio-economic relations that is different from the dominant ones; and this is the 'destabilization' most dangerous for that area, given that the forces of capitalism, even though distinct, are preeminent and decisive compared to the forces promoting parliamentary democracy. Thus, in the Western world, the destabilization of the former is perceived as more dangerous and unacceptable than the destabilization of the latter. It is in this sense that in Italy the truly 'destabilizing' factor is the PCI.

On the contrary, terrorism, in the form it has so far taken ('black', 'red', Arab) is not 'destabilizing'. It would become destabilizing if Italy were to move to the periphery of the system, weakening the defence mechanisms of the kind of society which currently exists. Yet, in its current form, terrorism does not threaten either the capitalist economy or parliamentary democracy. This statement can be explained by alluding to what *is immediately apparent* about terrorism, while leaving aside any hypothesis about the instigators, the colour or the goals of terrorist acts. In effect, even if we do not know who threw the stone that entered through the window, we can observe the damage it causes and the consequences it produces. That is to say that here, the *procedure* through which the thesis is reached is what matters (and the thesis might even be obvious); much less important is the thesis itself, separated from its justification.

Terrorism produces terror: in certain social categories when it is 'targeted' and strikes state officials, journalists, politicians, etc.; in the entire population when it is indiscriminate massacre. It is clear that terrorism produces terror in people only when people know about it, are informed of it and perceive it. *By showing,* by representing the destructive effects of terrorism, the mass media, especially television, *make terrorism seem real*: the terror of a few becomes, though with lesser intensity, the terror of tens of millions of people.

Terror increases the desire for security in people. In turn, this desire consolidates old habits and distances desires for change. When there is terror, people barricade themselves in their homes, reinforcing the old house: They do not go out to try to build a new house. Those who are afraid are also afraid, and especially afraid, of novelties. They defend themselves from fear by clinging to what is familiar – in private matters as in public ones. Therefore, those who are afraid do not look favourably on social changes, on the generous or ambitious proposals for societal renewal.

Now, given that changes and proposals for renewal form the very core of reformist and left-wing ideologies, when people are afraid, they instinctively withdraw their support for such ideologies or tend to reinterpret them in a more moderate sense. In this situation, the ideology in Italy that pays the highest price is that of the PCI, because it proposes the most radical and unpredictable renewal of society. In short, from terrorism comes fear, and from fear comes consolidation, i.e. the *stabilization* of the existing social, economic and political balances.

A further aspect of terrorism is visible to everyone – and yet, it is never underscored. In Italy, terrorism is *dosed*. If one accepts that an attack on a train has a relatively modest economic cost for the organizers and that the materials used (things and certain human types) are easily obtainable, it is a fact that terrorism, while capable of blowing up ten trains at once, only blows up one at a time, years apart. Terrorism does not develop all the destructive potential it presumably has. Thus, there is a *dosage* in the destruction and terror it seeks to produce.

The dosage is also noticeable from another fact: that so-called 'black' terrorism reaches its greatest intensity when so-called 'red' terrorism is significantly reduced; and vice versa. One can say that each intervenes when the other is not too noticeable. The alternation between 'black' and 'red' seems now to be itself alternating with Arab terrorism, which in recent times has had an intensity far higher than the 'traditional' one. One can track this entire game with the calendar in hand. If not 'preestablished', it is certainly an existing harmony.

Yet what would have happened if, in the Christmas of '84, ten trains had blown up? Is it an exaggeration to answer that martial law would have been imposed in Italy, the functions of the government would have concentrated in a restricted Committee with extraordinary powers, civil and parliamentary liberties would have been severely limited, and that the PCI, dragging the other left-wing forces with it, would have reacted violently to the possibility of being legally suffocated in the name of the superior national interest? These premises would have led to civil war and to the *destabilization* of our social system.

Ten trains blown up would have produced all this. But in the Christmas of '84 and at all other times, ten trains did not blow up. From Piazza Fontana and the murder of Aldo Moro to its 'Middle Eastern' forms, terrorism does not develop a destructiveness sufficient to dismantle the Italian social system but keeps it under constant pressure, expressing in a gradual and rationed fashion the destructive capacities of those exerting this pressure. And since, as has been said, terror diverts attention from the projects of societal renewal – especially those elaborated by the left – then *dosed* terrorism does not block and undoubtedly does not destroy, but rather *slows* down the emancipation of the masses led by the PCI.

This party is dismantling its Marxist–Leninist–Soviet ideology and, *at the same time*, is approaching power. Two processes. Nevertheless, the first has been, and still seems to be, slower than the second (that is, it has been and is still considered slower by the forces that safeguard the current structure of Italian society). In other words, the democratization of the PCI is slower than the formation of the conditions (electoral progress or electoral hold still alarming, penetration into society's structures, etc.) that allow the PCI to come to power. This means that if dosed terrorism slows down the emancipation of the masses led by the PCI, such terrorism slows the PCI's advance toward power, and thus *balances* these two processes (which form the current development of the PCI), i.e. it allows the democratization process of the PCI to gain ground compared to what is considered an overly rapid advance of the PCI toward power. As unsettling as this fact may seem, it must be faced: the immorality and illegality of dosed terror favour the democratization of the PCI. In the end, *also* (but not only) for this reason, democracy in Italy is 'induced' ['indotta', t/n] (with a closed 'o'–apart from whether it is also with an open 'o').[1]

If the instigators and the colour of terrorism are always controversial and not visible to everyone, what is visible to all is the persistent conviction of the PCI that indiscriminate massacres and even certain forms of 'red' terrorism are being orchestrated by the far-right. And of course, dosed terrorism would be consistent with a modern far-right project, which – as Max Weber already noted – regards democracy more consonant with the interests of capitalism than an authoritarian regime. But (aside from the issue of interpreting Arab terrorism) at this point, one must say that if the PCI's diagnosis were true, it would also be true that terrorism strikes Italian society because of the existence of the PCI. Hence, the PCI would have enormous responsibilities and would face a difficult problem to solve (which all Italian political forces, in any case, should be interested in solving). In effect, everyone condemns terrorism; but very few would be willing to blow themselves up for the sake of the PCI not wanting to slow down.

Yet, why should the PCI slow down? Why should the roots of terrorism not be eliminated instead? But can these roots really be eliminated? Or must a 'compromise' be reached instead that removes the *effects* in such a way as not to force their causes to reproduce them? In European democracies, the roots of terrorism are ultimately given by the same USA–USSR tension, that is, by the possibility that, to a varying degree, European capitalism becomes peripheral to the centre of the system and that, therefore, the two opposing systems use illegal means to favour, respectively, a centripetal and centrifugal direction in the behaviour of European states.

In addition, we find ourselves in a phase where Arab terrorism is still part of this game. Poor Arab countries are the least poor among the underdeveloped nations and can take on the role of leading the pressure that the poor countries exert (and will increasingly exert) on the rich ones. So far, it seems that this pressure may better serve the interests of the Soviet Union rather than those of the United States, since the USSR remains, after all, the state where the emancipation of the working classes from capitalist exploitation is still theorized and pursued. On the other hand, in the current intermediate phase, it is also possible that Arab terrorism – itself in a 'dosed' form – may have the same objective effects in a country like Italy as 'red' and 'black' terrorism, with regards to the balance in the development of the PCI, the democratization process and the process of moving closer to power. In this intermediate phase, eliminating the roots of terrorism would be like seeking to eliminate the very international framework of the USA–USSR conflict. The causes of terrorism cannot be eliminated (given the current conditions). Nonetheless, a 'compromise' – a series of 'compromises' – between the two opposing systems could be possible and may regulate disputes between them in a way that avoids resorting to terrorist violence.

Yet, in fact, this is an intermediate phase: it is unavoidable that underdeveloped countries will increasingly realize that the USSR belongs to the group of the rich countries of the Earth, and therefore, that it can never renounce its privileges in the name of the emancipation of the world proletariat. Faced with the growing pressure of the poor world on the rich world, it is therefore inevitable that internal conflicts within the rich world will lose significance, and that the opposing sides will prove willing to make reciprocal concessions that were once unthinkable: the USA and the USSR, labour and capital, demand for civil liberties and authoritarian state and ideology.

3

If we want to keep our feet on the ground – on the ground of democracy – it is not necessary to keep our head at the level of our feet though. I know that nowadays it is often considered a sign of seriousness to advocate for the feet. In fact, Thomas Mann said that he preferred the greyness of Anglo-Saxon democracy to the 'depth' of the German soul. But after one has busied oneself declaring our tastes and preferences, one is yet to see if reality is made in their image and likeness. In other words, the issue of the meaning of reality remains.

In the past, religious institutions have prevented the discussion of this issue, and nowadays political institutions have largely taken on this role. In the East, this is a blatant fact; in the West, it presents itself differently, in a less obvious and heavy way. Such difference is one component of the broader difference between real capitalism (and thus real democracy) and real socialism. But the difference between two objects does not exclude that they have something in common – and perhaps the essential thing.

It has often been stated that in Italy there is a tendency to forget one of the main aspects of democracy, whereby the government should be put in a position to govern and make decisions quickly, even if its electoral support is only 51 per cent of the votes.[2] That would involve adopting certain political engineering measures ['accorgimenti di ingegneria politica', t/n] that would make forms of obstructionism, such as those practised by the PCI concerning the government's sliding wage scale policies, impossible. Yet this thesis holds true for a 'pure' democracy, *in vitro*, for a democracy in the abstract ['da laboratorio', t/n]: not for what we can call 'real democracy' – in a similar sense to how 'real socialism' is referred to. In the abstract, the majority must be able to decide anything it wants, even with 51 per cent of the votes, for the minority will have to behave in the same way when it becomes the majority. Indeed, the possibility that opposing political forces alternate in power is the basis of the right for those who govern to make decisions independently of the minority and without being *paralysed by it*.

But, in fact, this is an abstract democracy. On the contrary, the 'real democracies' of the West prevent power, on point of principle, from being seized by communist or pro-Soviet forces – just as in the East it is categorically excluded, even more glaringly and emphatically, that Marxism–Leninism could be replaced by parliamentary democracy and a market economy.

One will reply that, in this way, 'real democracy' denies the fundamental democratic principle of the self-determination of peoples, according to which, if in the United States and the Western world the majority of people voted for pro-Soviet communism, one should bow even to that majority's will. Certainly. 'Real democracy' stands in contradiction to abstract democracy, or, if preferred, to the 'essence' of democracy. Yet our democracy is a democracy that is held back and fixed by the great forces of international capitalism to the current configuration of its will. And it would be very naive and dangerous to wish, in the name of the essence of democracy, this constraint to cease.[3]

I, too, prefer to live in this ailing democracy rather than in a totalitarian regime. But in stating this, I have merely expressed my own 'faith', in the broad yet also precise meaning of the word, according to which 'faith' refers to any knowledge or certainty (however absolute) that is not the destiny of truth – that is, the destiny that neither humans nor gods can deny or undermine: the Incontrovertible. Thus, 'faith' includes religious faith, modern science, common sense, historical forms of philosophy, mystical experience and political convictions.

Here again, of course, the form and content of religious faith are very different from those of scientific faith, yet they have this in common: neither is the Incontrovertible. Even though scientific faith may be regarded 'rational' compared to religious faith, they both remain at the same distance – that is, at an infinite distance – from the Incontrovertible (keeping in mind that incontrovertible truth could never be grasped as a product of the human brain, of the individual, of a social group, or of 'History').

Then, preferring democracy is a 'faith'. Even if we are well aware that democracy is a means of locomotion that may abandon us midway, we nonetheless have faith that by using it, there is at least the possibility of achieving some of our goals. Even if one is quite sceptical when taking a car instead of a train, one still places faith in the car. And it is also a form of faith to believe that the goals of democratic coexistence should be realized.

Thus, one encounters again the problem of the meaning of faith. This was discussed by a thinker as uncontroversial as Weber (uncontroversial to those who wish to engage with real and concrete issues). Yet if every faith is a *will* for the world to have one meaning rather than another, should one not say that *all* faiths are forms of *violence* and that resorting to any faith, even to free humanity from violence, is like trying to cure poisoning by ingesting a different kind of poison?

4

One often says that the PCI can only come to power if it stops being a communist party and transforms itself from a revolutionary Marxist force into a reformist social–democratic one. I have been repeating this in detail for a long time, so I am pleased that many have taken up this idea. Nevertheless, the crucial question concerns *the reasons* behind the transformation currently underway within the PCI.

In recent years, there has certainly been ongoing discussion about the PCI's evolution towards social democracy. Yet this has been discussed, and it is still discussed, within inadequate conceptual frameworks. For example, this evolution is often understood as a contingent development, as a 'fact' to be observed (as something happening, or just beginning, or well under way); or as a tendency that can be observed by statistical-probabilistic sciences; alternatively, the evolution of the PCI is seen as a project that requires, above all, the 'good will' of European communists to be realized. But Western democratic culture is also able to acknowledge that 'facts' can be replaced by other facts that move in the opposite direction, that probabilistic diagnoses are unreliable in such a complex matter, and that the road to hell is paved with good intentions ['l'inferno è lastricato di buone intenzioni', t/n].[4] The conclusion is: the usual way of considering the evolution of communism towards social democracy does not yet manage to dispel the suspicions that the capitalist world harbours toward European communist movements. Nonetheless, the transformation of the PCI belongs to a much broader scenario, to a global process in which revolutions are 'destined' to turn into reforms and social engineering, and in which conceptual and operational structures of a 'philosophical' kind (such as Marxist-inspired communism) are 'destined' to turn into scientific conceptual and operational structures. It is precisely in relation to such 'destiny' (see Chapters 2 and 3) that the thesis in my writings – 'Italian communism (but not just Italian communism) is transforming into reformist social democracy, guided by a scientific-technological approach' – fundamentally differs from all the analyses of the PCI's evolution and of global communism that, on the surface, seem to be saying the same thing.

To state that traditional civilization and its philosophical-religious forms are 'destined' to fade into scientific-technological civilization is to state that the criticisms directed at tradition by contemporary culture (and Marxism, like Christianity, now belongs to tradition) are simply the external form, the semblance, the altered phenomenon of this 'destination'. In effect, this word alludes to the fact of true inevitability and necessity, to which today's dominant form of knowledge is entirely foreign, given that it is essentially reducible to scientific knowledge (and to true inevitability and necessity the traditional understanding of the inevitable and the necessary is equally foreign). Science knows (science believes it knows) how to dominate the world, but it does not know how to 'pre-destine' the world to anything.[5]

In the early 1920s, in the opening essay of *History and Class Consciousness*, György Lukács argued that the application of the method of natural sciences to social reality significantly contributes to the transformation of revolutionary communism into reformist or revisionist social democracy. This is one of the most important and consequential pages in the entire history of theoretical Marxism – one of the crucial moments in how Marxism has responded to the attempt by social-democratic culture to render it irrelevant.

Lukács claims that according to natural sciences, it is indisputable that the reality they refer to (namely, nature) contains and can contain no 'contradiction'. For instance, the same body cannot be simultaneously at rest and in motion in relation to the same frame of reference. If scientific theories encounter a contradiction, this fact cannot indicate an 'imperfection of reality' but rather an 'imperfection of scientific knowledge' of reality. Therefore, to remove this imperfection, it is not reality that must be changed but the scientific knowledge of it.

Now – and here lies the core of Lukács' argument – if this methodological approach of the natural sciences is applied to society, the possibility of conceiving of society as something that can or should be changed is lost. In this application, indeed, even the 'contradictions' encountered by the social sciences would need to be grasped not as imperfections of society but as imperfections of the scientific knowledge of it. And in this case, too, to eliminate such contradictions, it would suffice to correct the scientific theories that investigate social reality rather than modifying social reality itself. This circumstance helps capitalist society distance itself from the spectre of revolution. Indeed, for Marx, 'revolution' is precisely the 'real' transformation of society and not simply an edifying intellectual exercise ['atto di igiene mentale', t/n].

Lukács notes that this application of the natural sciences methodological approach to society is not only typical of capitalist economic science but also of the social-democratic economics of his time, such as Bernstein's 'revisionism' and Hilferding's 'Austro–Marxism'. Social democracy and the application of the scientific method to society go hand in hand. In that way, the fundamental structure of society remains untouched. Only minor adjustments are permitted.

Referring back to Marx, Lukács asserts the necessity of considering society differently from nature: the contradictions that emerge in a genuine understanding of society, especially of capitalist society, are not signs of an imperfect state of our scientific knowledge but 'inseparably belong to the essence of reality itself, to the essence of capitalist society'. Marx's work consists precisely in attempting to show that contradiction, or rather, the extreme form of contradiction, belongs to the 'reality' represented by capitalist society and that 'revolution' is the fundamental act of practical philosophy, tasked with 'really suppressing' the contradictions of social reality. Therefore, according to Lukács, in socialist reflection on capitalism, abandoning the method of Marx's (that is, Hegel's) philosophy for the method of the natural sciences is a particularly significant aspect of socialism's submission to capitalism and of the reformist social-democratic renunciation of revolution. Thus, one must go back to Marx. The social-democratic illness can be cured, and the proletariat can confidently prepare for revolution.

On the other hand, it was Lukács himself, in this passage, who provided the most substantial basis for critics of Marxism who are unwilling to place limits on science to label Marxism as irrationalism. In effect, by claiming that capitalist 'reality' is contradiction, Marxism contradicts the fundamental principle of science: that 'principle of non-contradiction' inherited by science from Aristotelian philosophy, which categorically excludes the possibility that reality itself is contradictory (for instance, that a body could be simultaneously at rest and in motion). Followed by a crowd of imitators, K. Popper and H. Kelsen were the first to make this criticism. Rarely up to the challenge, crowds of imitators have also referred to this passage of Lukács. Yet the Popper–Kelsen criticism seems both effective and an extremely quick way to dispose of Marx, precisely because Marx's aim to demonstrate that capitalist 'reality' is contradiction would attempt to demonstrate the impossible. In that way, one can spare oneself the effort of following this demonstration step by step.

According to this criticism, Marx has confused the logical concept of 'contradiction' with the concepts of 'antagonism' or 'conflict' between social classes. Therefore, it is not a matter of making a revolution in order to eliminate a contradiction that does not and cannot exist. Rather, it is a matter of supporting one or another of the forces at play. Thus, taking a stand with socialism becomes a 'moral task' (for those who take it up). Social democracy has its ultimate foundation in this moral principle. (Capitalism may respond that its moral duty is to defend capital and profit.)

It is undisputable that Lukács himself has facilitated Popper's and Kelsen's criticism by giving the impression that the 'contradictions' whose reality is categorically excluded by the natural sciences are the same as the 'contradictions' inherent into capitalist society. But they are not the same thing. Indeed, in the first case, 'contradiction' refers to that whose reality is impossible; on the contrary, in the second case, 'contradiction' refers to the 'act of contradicting' ['l'atto del contraddirsi', t/n]. After all, while it is impossible for reality to be contradictory, it is in fact possible to contradict oneself: and it is not only individuals who can contradict themselves but even groups, social institutions and society as a whole. Thus, Marx does not deny the 'principle of non-contradiction' but instead claims (whether rightly or wrongly is another matter) that capitalist society represents the most gigantic negation of this principle. For Marx, then, destroying capitalism is the supreme rational act. Therefore, the anti-Marxist criticism of Popper and Kelsen fails to show the inevitability of transforming revolutionary communism into reformist social democracy.[6]

The confusion between the 'act of contradicting oneself' and the 'contradictoriness of reality' (i.e. between erring ['l'errare', t/n], which can be real, and error ['l'errore', t/n], which cannot be real) is present even beyond the boundaries of anti-Marxist polemics. Indeed, the latest developments of sociological 'functionalism' claim that, since functions contradictory to each other exist within society, sociology must adopt a 'non-Aristotelian' logic, which rejects the unconditional value of the 'principle of non-contradiction'. Popper and Kelsen argue that since this principle is undeniable, contradiction cannot be real; on its part, neofunctionalism (e.g. N. Luhmann) responds that, since the contradiction between social functions is real, this principle must be set aside through the introduction of so-called 'many-valued logics' (which allow for intermediate values between 'true' and 'false').

Whatever opinion one might hold about the relationship between these logics and the 'principle of non-contradiction', there can be no doubt that both Popper and Kelsen (and their followers), on one hand, and on the other hand, neofunctionalism, reach opposite conclusions starting from the same misunderstanding: the notion that the existence of social contradictions entails the 'contradictoriness of reality', that is, the negation of the 'principle of non-contradiction'. On the contrary, even social functions that contradict each other simply represent a 'contradicting oneself', for the occurrence of which there is no need to invoke 'non-Aristotelian logics'. Even psychoanalysis deals with 'contradicting oneself' when it affirms that logical laws do not apply to the unconscious and that 'this is especially true for the law of contradiction' (Freud, *Introduction to Psychoanalysis*, 1933).

For about a century, social–democratic culture has been trying to distance itself from revolutionary Marxist philosophy, criticizing it in the name of science. However, each time, the criticism has fallen flat, and thus the shift from Marxism to social democracy has never been conclusive. After all, how can a scientific criticism of philosophy be conclusive if scientific logic, by its nature, rules out being conclusive? In this circumstance, the struggle between Marxism and social democracy, and, more broadly, between tradition and current forms of Western culture, is resolved on a practical level, that is, in relation to the practical ability of the opposing forces to prevail over one another. There is still a long way to go before it becomes evident that Marxism is 'destined' to dissolve into science and social-democratic reformism – according to the meaning of 'destiny' (see Chapter 1) that Western culture has not yet reached but may reach, and which, at any rate, is essentially different from the 'destiny' found in the gaze of the destiny of truth.

5

One argues that the thought of Piero Sraffa is not just a mandatory step in contemporary economics, but that it has overthrown neoclassical economic theory, i.e. the theoretical foundations of capitalist economics, and that it has confirmed the essential theses of Marx, in which the classical phase of economic science (Smith, Ricardo) culminates.

On the opposite side, one claims that Marx's dependence on Hegelian dialectics removes all scientific value from Marx's analysis, because dialectics is the negation of the very fundamental principle of scientific knowledge, the 'principle of non-contradiction'. It is evident that Kelsen and Popper, drawing on Kant, have pioneered this kind of criticism.[7]

It is a matter of understanding the essence of dialectics, which Marx inherits from Hegel. It is a matter of understanding the relationship between 'intellect' and 'reason' in Hegel. I briefly recall here what is discussed analytically in several of my writings, particularly in *The Originary Structure*.

The intellect – which considers various aspects of reality as separate from one another, autonomous, subsisting in themselves – is a poor way of adhering to the principle of non-contradiction. In order to prevent opposites from mixing and, for example, good from mixing with evil, the intellect ends up thinking that there is no relationship whatsoever between good and evil, and that good exists entirely in itself, absolutely separate from evil.

Yet, according to Hegel, it is precisely this separation – i.e. the activity of the intellect – that is the root of contradiction. Being absolutely isolated from evil, good cannot even be thought of as the negation of evil – because, in order to negate and overcome evil, good must necessarily relate to evil and even come into contact with it. A good that is not the negation of evil presents itself as evil; it contradicts itself. Therefore, every content of the intellect is contradictory.

Nevertheless, Hegel also shows that reason is the overcoming of the contradictions of the intellect. Reason conceives of the *unity*, the *relationship* of the different and opposed aspects of reality. Reason negates the intellect, i.e. it uproots the root of contradiction. By conceiving of the unity and relationship of the opposites (for instance, good and evil), reason does not affirm that the opposites are identical (it does not claim that good is evil); on the contrary, reason is the fundamental condition thanks to which opposites can remain opposites and not blend with one another. Therefore, according to Hegel, reason does not negate the principle of non-contradiction, but its misuse – the use the intellect makes of it, which leads to the contradiction of all its contents.[8]

As we know, the criticism Popper and Kelsen (followed by many others) direct at Marx on this point is that Marx denies this principle because for him capitalist reality is a contradiction; while the principle of non-contradiction exists to deny that any reality can be contradictory.

Yet, Marx cannot be dismissed in that way, because according to him, 'contradiction' is something that belongs to capitalism insofar as capitalism is a *way of thinking*, precisely the way of thinking in which the intellect consists, separating the various aspects of the world. And while the principle of non-contradiction denies that reality can be contradictory, it certainly does not deny that thinking can contradict itself. (Naturally, capitalism, for Marx, is not only a way of thinking, but an action that is guided by a certain way of thinking and, therefore, an action that seeks to realize the separation of the worker from nature and the means of production. It seeks to realize the contradiction without being able to succeed in doing so.)[9]

Perhaps, *coquetry* can help Popperians understand Hegel and Marx. The infinite nuances of feminine coquetry! Among its most recognizable traits is the sidelong glance paired with a half-turned head. A look that is not a look, a granting that is a withholding, a 'contemporaneity of yes and no', as Georg Simmel wrote at the start of the century in his pages on *Fashion*.[10] He had in mind the coquetry of the Art Nouveau woman, who mastered the delightful secrets of 'giving and taking away at the same time' and of ensuring that these two opposing attitudes 'are both perceived in the same instant'.

Yet *coquetry* plays with reality; it does not take any of the opposites it uses in its game seriously. Even though Simmel does not explicitly mention this, the game is precisely what prevents something as delightful as coquetry from being confused with something as lacking in charm as madness. For if, as Simmel states, the 'general formula of coquetry' is the 'contemporaneity of yes and no', this is also the general formula of contradiction, and the root of madness is precisely contradiction. In mediocre madness, the contradiction is obvious, everyone sees it; on the other hand, in great madness the contradiction is hidden, disguised as wisdom. In an analogous fashion, in vulgar coquetry, the contradiction is obvious, while in refined coquetry, contradiction is masked by behaviour. But as a matter of fact, the coquette plays with their own contradiction, while the madman takes it seriously.

It is clear that the contradiction of the coquette is just their way of feeling and thinking. The coquette wants to make others believe they are simultaneously a yes and a no, but they can never truly be so. They will succeed in glancing sideways and turning their head, but they cannot look both crooked and straight at the same time, keeping their head forward and turned at once. In the nature of things ['nelle cose', t/n], there is no 'contemporaneity of yes and no' and with regards to this nature, what the coquette wants to make others believe is a consciously acted out dream.

In a similar fashion, the contradiction, of which a madman is convinced, does not exist in reality: it is only their way of thinking, a dream; although, undoubtedly, the madman's body and the chair they sit on when they believe they are Julius Caesar on the steps of the Forum are not a dream.

With the necessary precautions, this is the direction in which one must interpret Marx's thesis (be this true or false) that capitalism is 'madness' and 'contradiction'. If it is, then the content of madness and contradiction respectively, like the content of any other madness and contradiction, does not really exist: it is a dream, a way of thinking, just like the ravings of a madman and the yes and no of a coquette. Nevertheless, just as the body and chair of the madman, and the glances of the coquette, are not dreams, neither is the actual reality (work, factories, circulation of goods and capital) that capitalism considers and arranges according to its own way of thinking. This way of thinking is a contradiction, a mistake that, as happens with the coquette and the madman, tries to actualize itself, believing it will succeed. Of course – let us repeat – according to Marx, capitalism is not just a way of thinking. Just as coquetry and madness are not. Yet, always for Marx, within the context of capitalist economy, commodities are 'forms of thought' (*Gedankenformen*); and certainly, they are 'objective' forms of thought (*Capital*, Chapter 1, first edition) – just as that person's sitting on the chair is the 'objectification' of their belief that they are Caesar in the Forum (keeping in mind that the 'mad form', as Marx calls it, of the real and material structures of capitalism is considerably more complex than that person's belief that they are Caesar).

Yet precisely for this reason, one must defend the coquette and the mad from certain scholars who are rather fixated. According to these scholars, the coquette and the mad (but the list is much longer) do not exist because the only contradictions possible 'are those that can arise in scientific theories' (as the Popperians repeat).[11] Lukács clearly showed that such claim prevents us from seeing the contradictions of society and is therefore a good way to avoid transforming it; a method that replaces revolution with the theoretical correction of an error.

Given that they are followers of K. Popper, we might call these scholars 'the Popperians' – strange pro-capitalists who do not even recognize the dignity of real capitalism (that is, what capitalists *do*) as a 'theory', a way of thinking, in addition to iron, cotton and moving capital. If invited to discuss the topic, the Popperians would argue that since coquetry is a contradiction, anyone who admits its existence is asserting that reality is contradictory, i.e. that it contradicts the principle of non-contradiction, the supreme principle of science. And given that even madmen contradict themselves, the Popperians would say that the psychiatrists who try to cure them are recognizing the reality of contradiction and are therefore also going against the supreme principle of science.

Generally speaking, as seen above, the Popperians prefer another example: Marx claims that capitalism is a contradiction; therefore, he claims that there exists a reality – capitalism, indeed – that violates the supreme principle of science. According to the Popperians, then, coquettes and madmen do not exist: they are contradictory realities. And neither does capitalism exist if, with Marx, one believes that capitalism is but contradiction and madness. (Even though, for Popper, even 'facts' are theories and, therefore, like coquettes, they can contradict themselves, this does not seem to bother Popper or, much less, the Popperians.) At this point, the coquette, the mad and capitalism can only apologize to the Popperians for the fact that they exist. And from the Popperians we learn this strange affair: that the principle of non-contradiction does not only deny that reality is contradictory, but it also denies that humans and social institutions can contradict themselves.

But once one leaves behind Popper's, Kelsen's, and their followers' inability to control the functioning of the principle of non-contradiction, a real issue of exceptional significance emerges, one of which these scholars (and not just them) are completely unaware, like children who have accidentally leaned against the wall beyond which lies a treasure and the wild beasts guarding it. In a passage from the *Book IV* of *Metaphysics*, as renowned as it is little understood (1005b 6–34), Aristotle shows that the *principium firmissimum* (indeed, what will later be called the 'principle of non-contradiction') not only excludes that reality can be contradictory but also that humans can be convinced of contradiction, and therefore that contradicting oneself can be real. The exceptional interest of this theme is that according to Aristotle, it is the very first principle that excludes the realization of the thought denying it. This time, the coquettes, the mad, and all those who contradict themselves (individuals or institutions) really have something to fear for their existence. The resolution of this aporia – the resolution that, therefore, equates to the deduction of the possibility of erring – is indicated in the 'Additional Part' of *The Essence of Nihilism* (see pp. 313–34). In the present context, though, one can only say that this theme lies at a level that the kind of investigation developed by the aforementioned scholars entirely misses.

7

Summary: The West as the history of nihilism

1

Ancient Greek philosophy says something never heard before in the history of humanity. And it says it once and for all. It says that things oscillate between being and nothingness. In effect, it is Ancient Greek philosophy that expresses, for the first time, the infinite opposition between being and nothingness; that is, it speaks of nothingness as absolute negativity: *tò pántos mè ón* (Plato, *Civitas*, 478 d): *nihil absolutum*. Precisely because it brings to light the infinite opposition between being and nothingness, Ancient Greek philosophy can assert that the things of the world oscillate between being and nothingness. That is, they come out of nothingness and return to it. This oscillation is not just a property of the things of the world: it is their very essence. And precisely because of their relation to being and nothingness, things are called by the Ancient Greeks 'beings', *ónta*.

In the *Republic* (*Civitas*, 479 c), Plato indicates the oscillation between being and nothingness with the word *epamphoterízein*. The things, *qua* beings, are a 'struggling' (*erízein*) 'between' (*epí*) 'the one and the other' (*amphótera*), that is, between being and nothingness. In the *Republic*, Plato refers to the beings of the world; yet Ancient Greek philosophy, and later the entire Western metaphysical tradition, also affirms the existence of beings that are immutable and eternal – first and foremost, it affirms the eternity and immutability of God, i.e. it affirms that God does *not* oscillate between being and nothingness. But when the philosophical tradition asserts the immutability and eternity of the divine being, immutability and eternity are not ascribed to God because God is a being, but because God is *a certain being*, different from the others, privileged compared to the others. For if one were to affirm that God is eternal and immutable *because God is a being*, eternity and immutability would have to be affirmed *of every being*. That is to say that, according to the tradition – and later, to all Western thought – *beings, qua beings* (beings, considered as to its pure being beings ['quanto al suo puro esser ente', t/n]) may not be: it can oscillate between being and nothingness, there is nothing in it that prevents such oscillation. In that sense, even in Ancient Greek thought, the oscillation between being and nothingness is not something that simply regards the things of the world: oscillation is the essence of beings *qua* beings, it concerns every being (even if Aristotle tries to support the thesis that beings *qua* beings can realize themselves either as becoming being or as immutable being). For Ancient Greek philosophy, a thing, as such, is that which *becomes*, that is, it comes from its having been nothing and returns to its being nothing. It oscillates between being and nothingness. Contrary to what continues to be repeated, *first of all*, Plato is the evoker and guardian of becoming, that is, of the dominant category of modern and particularly of contemporary culture. *Becoming* (history, time), in the name of which every form of anti-Platonism speaks, was first brought to light by Ancient Greek thought, which gathers around Plato as its centre. (Even Parmenides is able to affirm the illusory character of becoming, precisely because even Parmenides – first among Ancient Greek philosophers – defines becoming as the oscillation of beings between being and nothingness.)

For a long time, in my writings, I have sought to show that the Ancient Greek meaning of being – that is, the 'thing' as an oscillation between being and nothingness – is the dimension that gathers and unifies the infinite multiplicity of events and structures in which Europe and the entire Western civilization consist. And for a long time, in my writings, I have sought to show that in the Ancient Greek meaning of being lies the extreme alienation, the extreme distance from truth – that is, the persuasion that things, beings, are nothing. According to the entire Western civilization, the Ancient Greek meaning of being is the originary and fundamental self-evidence; yet what the West feels as originary self-evidence is in truth extreme folly: the persuasion that beings, *qua* beings, are nothing. Therefore, the Ancient Greek meaning of being is *nihilism* in its most hidden and radical meaning. Precisely for this reason, one must state that the West is the history of nihilism – therefore, in a sense which is entirely different from the sense of Nietzsche and Heidegger. In fact, even Nietzsche and Heidegger remain completely within the Ancient Greek, Platonic persuasion that beings are becoming ['che l'ente sia divenire', t/n], they are an oscillation between being and nothingness.

The entire Western culture misses the essential meaning of nihilism, because it is necessarily linked to what is the supreme self-evidence according to the West: the becoming of things. Certainly, even from the perspective of Western culture, nihilism is the attitude that treats as nothing what for this culture is something positive. For example, for Jacobi, idealism is nihilism, because according to idealism, reality, which (for Jacobi) is independent of thought, is nothing; for Nietzsche, Christian nihilism treats the things of the Earth as nothing; for Heidegger, scientific nihilism treats as nothing the specific and qualitative concreteness of things, and the nihilism of the West treats as nothing the 'Being' of beings ['l'"Essere" dell'ente', t/n], taking into account only beings. Yet the 'leaving aside' and 'sacrificing' (*Preisgeben*) of the concreteness of things, alluded to by Heidegger, corresponds to the 'abstraction' alluded to by Hegel and Marx: Indeed, even Hegel could say that abstract intellect is nihilism because it 'leaves aside', that is, it abstracts from what is essentially united to what the abstract intellect considers; and after all, even Marx could say that capitalism is nihilism for it leaves aside, it abstracts, that is, treats as nothing the specific concreteness of human labours, i.e. their real inequality.

Nevertheless, in all these cases, the point of view that is identified as nihilism is a persuasion that posits as nothing what for that persuasion is already nothing – not what for that persuasion is a being. For instance, according to idealism, a reality independent of thought is an absurdity, that is, it is nothing; so that idealism, denying the existence of such a reality, affirms that nothing is nothing, not that beings are nothing. On the contrary, nihilism, in its essential and profoundly hidden meaning – that kind of nihilism which is hidden in the belief in the existence of becoming – is the persuasion in which *beings*, *qua* beings, are affirmed to be nothing. In its essence, nihilism is profoundly more radical than any attempt, made by philosophical thought, to affirm the mixture of being and nothingness. To think that beings come from nothingness and return to it means to think – without realizing it, but in an absolute way – that beings are nothingness. In that sense, nihilism is the unconscious of the West, an unconscious that *in a reversed form* manifests itself in the different ways in which the West *rejects* the identification of beings and nothingness; and above all, the unconscious manifests itself in that form of rejection of the nothingness of beings, which is called the 'principle of non-contradiction'. Even Hegel never intended to argue that beings are nothingness. Yet, it is precisely in the way in which Western culture affirms the opposition of beings to nothingness that the extreme folly lies, that is, the implicit, unconscious persuasion that beings are nothing.

2

The way in which Ancient Greek philosophy conceives of the meaning of beings launches the dimension in which the entire Western history develops. Not only the history of Western culture, but the history itself of the Western civilization.

Thus, the Ancient Greek meaning of being is at the root of every possible European cultural identity. Along with others, Latin culture and Germanic tradition, Christianity and modern science are the great forms in which that meaning manifests itself. The persuasion – the belief – that the birth and death of things are the coming out of things from nothingness and their return to it forms the background against which the forms of Ancient Greek and Latin culture, the Roman sense of the State, Christianity, theological reflection, from the Church Fathers to the Protestant Reformation, biblical texts and faith, the political–legal structures of European society, the mechanisms that govern the formation of European national languages, artistic forms, the entire development of philosophical thought (and thus the interpretation of being as subjectivity, thinking, action, language), logical–mathematical–linguistic sciences, the configuration of the economy, ideologies and revolutions in the West, modern science all take shape. The current planetary reach of the civilization of technics, which takes shape in the recent centuries of European history, is the perfect expression of the Ancient Greek meaning of being. In fact, the will to dominate things reaches its extreme possibilities only when things are understood as oscillating between being and nothingness, that is, as available to the forces that push them into being and into nothingness. The Ancient Greek faith in the oscillation of beings unleashes the extreme form of the will to power (i.e. a form which could not have formed before the Ancient Greek evocation of becoming); and the civilization of technics is the culmination of this extreme form of the will to power.

However, the will to power can only want to dominate the world if, first of all, it wants the world to exist, that is, the dimension of what-is-to-be-dominated. One can want the transformation of the world only if, first, one believes – that is, wants – that the state in which the world finds itself is flexible and dissoluble. Believing, that is, wanting that things oscillate between being and nothingness, Ancient Greek philosophy dissolves the bonds that unite things to being and nothingness, and thus posits the extreme flexibility and dissolubility of the world. The belief in the existence of becoming is the originary form of the will to power.

Thus, with Ancient Greek thought, the most radical and peremptory form of praxis comes to light: the one in which one believes that things can be made to come out of nothingness and return to it. The demiurge god and the creator god bring form, or both form and matter, into being, by making them come out of nothingness: the Demiurge and the Creator are the first great form of technical domination over the world – Plato (*Sophist*, 275 e) speaks precisely of *theia techne*. The civilization of technics is the last great form of theological domination over the world. All forms of philosophical thought that, like Heidegger's, reject the civilization of technics, do not realize that they move, just like technics, within the Ancient Greek meaning of being and delude themselves into thinking that they can escape the consequences that unavoidably arise from that meaning – consequences which the civilization of technics is developing in the most rigorous way. If in Western civilization the originary form of the will to power is represented by the belief that becoming (history, time) exists, that is, that beings are an oscillation between being and nothingness, every criticism that Western culture makes of the will to power remains internal to the originary form of the will to power while trying to avoid what inevitably arises from that originary form. In effect, if beings are entities which oscillate between being and nothingness, then it belongs to the very essence of beings to be produced, destroyed, created, annihilated, manipulated, transformed, devastated, controlled, dominated, exploited without limit. As a matter of fact, a limit would stop the oscillation of beings. The faith in the existence of becoming, i.e. in the existence of the oscillation of beings, is faith in the susceptibility to being dominated ['dominabilità', t/n] of beings and therefore in the existence of the forces that contest the domination of beings. The struggle in which these forces clash is itself an aspect, or rather, by now, an emerging aspect of becoming. The scientific–technological organization of the world is now the force that subordinates every other force to itself. More than any other, such force is able to push the oscillation of beings to its extreme.

3

Yet the belief in the existence of becoming is *at once* the originary form of the will to power and the opening of the extreme *threat*. What is threatened is the very will to power. At the beginning of the West, the will to power endangers itself in an extreme way precisely with the act in which it establishes the originary condition for its power. If one believes that things (events, forms, situations, aspects, functions) come out of nothingness and return to it, becoming presents itself as the irruption of the absolutely unpredictable and unexpected. Before the Ancient Greek evocation of the meaning of becoming, things did not present themselves as that which comes out of nothing, so their unpredictability was irrelevant. Myth anticipates the substance of everything that happens. But that which comes out of nothingness, that which has nothing behind it, is *absolutely* unpredictable. Nothingness is nothing ['il niente è niente', t/n], meaning that in nothingness there is nothing to be predicted. And the absolute unpredictability of that which comes from nothingness is the root of anguish and terror. Therefore, anguish and terror belong to the essence of the will to power.

To this essence also belongs the will for salvation, for what irrupts from nothingness jeopardizes the survival of the will to power. In order to ward off what threatens it, the will to power must predict the unpredictable (cf. above, Chapter 1, sections 9 et seq.). No barrier holds if the nature of the forces pressing upon it is not predicted. In fact, prediction is the originary barrier against the threat of becoming. From the very beginning, Ancient Greek philosophy conceives of itself as *theoria*: pure and disinterested contemplation. Yet, *theoria* satisfies the fundamental interest of the will to power: it satisfies the will for salvation. In effect, like myth, philosophical *theoria* anticipates, and therefore predicts, the substance of everything that comes to pass. Yet Ancient Greek thought finds itself before the *extreme* unpredictability and threat of that which comes from nothingness, and so, unlike myth, the Ancient Greeks build a *theoria* that aims to serve as the incontrovertible and definitive prediction of the meaning of the world. According to Ancient Greek thought, the remedy and the shelter from the extreme threat of the oscillation of beings is *epistéme*: the vision of the definitive Meaning of the world, which 'stands' (*–stéme*) firm, imposing itself 'on' (*epí*) everything that comes from nothing and 'on' every negation that seeks to undermine the standing of *epistéme*. Within *epistéme*, the definitive Meaning of the world is the immutable and the divine from which all things come and to which they return in their oscillation between being and nothingness. Things are always an emergence from nothingness and a return to it, but that which is essential and indispensable in them pre-exists and is preserved in the ground and in the divine meaning of the world revealed by *epistéme*.

The *epistéme* is the dimension within which all the immutables and eternals of the West are erected: God, the spiritual soul, the natural law that guides moral, legal and social behaviour, the various forms of economic life, conceived as eternal natural laws (for instance, in the eyes of early capitalism, the market economy is a natural and therefore unalterable condition of human life), the laws of physical nature, natural beauty and its role as the principle of artistic expression, absolute principles and truths. There is more. The incontrovertibility and definitiveness of *epistéme* poses itself as the model by which Christian faith itself conceives of itself. Indeed, it is true that Christian faith does not seek to show epistemically (i.e. through the 'natural light' of reason) the incontrovertibility of its content, but it still seeks to be an incontrovertible and definitive knowledge, in effect the supreme form of incontrovertibility and definitiveness, which stands even above *epistéme* and measures its value and claims. Christian faith is the heir of the will for truth in which *epistéme* consists. Unlike *epistéme*, Christian faith can address the masses and free them from the terror of becoming, but in such salvation, Christian faith develops and reintroduces the fundamental structure of Ancient Greek philosophy: saving oneself from the oscillation of beings through the incontrovertible, definitive and absolute evocation of the definitive Meaning of reality, to which everything that irrupts into existence from nothingness must conform.

4

At the beginning of the West, the will to power evokes the extreme threat – the oscillation between being and nothingness – and, at the same time, it evokes the first great form of shelter, remedy and salvation. The shelter is true knowledge, i.e. incontrovertible and stable knowledge (*epistéme*), in which the definitive Meaning of the world reveals itself, along with its articulation in the various aspects of nature and human existence. To know the true Meaning of the world means to predict the unpredictability of what comes from nothingness. Prediction is anticipation, *ante-capere*, that is, the originary way of mastering the world, the foundation of all possible domination. Therefore, the evocation of the immutable is a remedy against the terror of becoming and, at the same time, a means of dominating the world.

The evocation of the immutables and their destruction form the two epochs in which the history of the West unfolds: the epoch of tradition and the epoch of modernity. Two conflicting ways of preparing the remedy against the threat and terror of becoming. In an increasingly radical fashion, modern Europe realizes that the evocation of the immutables ends up making the becoming of reality unthinkable, that is, it ends up making unthinkable the very dimension that pushes towards the evocation of the immutables. If the incontrovertible and definitive Meaning of the world anticipates events, becoming becomes mere appearance. Yet the belief in the existence of becoming, that is, the oscillation of beings between being and nothingness, conceives of the existence of becoming as an originary, fundamental *self-evidence* (and it is primarily within *epistéme* that this belief takes form). Thus, realizing that the immutables make becoming unthinkable, modern Europe sees in them the denial of the self-evidence of any self-evidence, that is, a mere claim and illusion of immutability which must therefore be destroyed. The gigantic phenomenon of *liberation* of the modern human is the process of liberation *from the immutables* that dominate in the tradition of the West. The destruction of feudal society and culture by the bourgeoisie and the Renaissance culture, the Protestant rejection of the hierarchy of the Roman Church and its theological interpretation of the Bible, the rejection of philosophical *epistéme* by bourgeois society, of Christianity and modern science, the great bourgeois and communist revolutions, the progressive distancing of European and Western masses from Christianity, the ever more radical rejection of any incontrovertible truth within philosophical and scientific knowledge, the distancing of art from traditional canons of beauty and of the realistic representation of the world, the subordination of capitalist and socialist ideology to the scientific–technological organization of existence – these are the great forms in which the destruction of the immutables manifests itself in modern Europe and the West.

This is not just a will to destroy, but the awareness that – according to Nietzsche's expression – the remedy has been worse than the evil. Nevertheless, this awareness struggles towards acknowledging (but is not incapable of acknowledging) that the evocation and destruction of the immutables show their authentic meaning only in their connection with Ancient Greek ontology. However, such an awareness is not capable of understanding that the belief in becoming is the belief and the originary form of the will to power. Indeed, every awareness and consciousness that the West has of itself takes shape and develops within that belief, which, in the eyes of the West (that is, of itself), presents itself as the supreme and indisputable self-evidence. Thus, the West can only grasp certain aspects of the structure of the evocation and destruction of the immutables. This structure can be – once again – summed up as follows.

Precisely because the immutable anticipates in itself the essence and substance of everything that in becoming comes from nothingness and is therefore the law and the rule to which everything that emerges must conform, for this very reason, the coming from nothingness and the absolute unpredictability of what was nothingness become mere appearance, illusion. In order to be powerful, the will to power evokes becoming – the belief in the evocation of becoming is thus the fundamental condition of power. On the other hand, the immutable, with which the will to power defends itself from the threat of becoming, and which the will to power itself has evoked, makes becoming illusory and, therefore, makes the very originary form of the will to power illusory. At this point, the terror caused by the domination of the immutable over becoming becomes more unbearable than the terror caused by becoming itself. Indeed, the will to power stifles and denies itself. The human being feels suffocated. ('Human being'–this is the most decisive of the names with which the will to power calls itself.) Modern civilization is the process of liberation from this contradiction, where the will to power turns against itself, prediction erases the unpredictability in which becoming consists, and (cf. above, Chapter 1, sections 6–10) nothingness is entified. And the contradiction is solved precisely through the ever more radical and extensive destruction of the immutables that dominate the history of the West.

After the attempts of philosophy and Christianity, it is modern science that presents itself as the effective remedy against the threat of becoming. In order not to be worse than the evil, the remedy must be a prediction that does not erase the unpredictability of nothingness from which things come. Certainly, this implies a new way of existing, where life loses its most terrifying aspects for humans, and where humans feel attracted by adventure and risk.

The prediction that does not erase the unpredictability of nothingness is a prediction that *works* but does not have any knowledge that guarantees its functioning incontrovertibly. It is a prediction open to be disproved by the becoming of reality, and thus is a hypothetical prediction. The experimental method of modern science is precisely such effective and functional prediction of the unpredictability of the world. Although modern science tends to forget about its roots in the Ancient Greek evocation of the oscillation of beings, the progressive transformation of scientific laws into probabilistic laws, and thus the growing affirmation in science of the casual nature of events, indicates that no immutable rule or law can push nothingness into becoming a being, following one direction rather than another. Precisely because nothingness is nothing ['il niente è niente', t/n], the world happens by chance. Now, the only way to predict chance is the formulation of statistical–probabilistic predictions. While ensuring a level of dominance over the world never before reached, such predictions do not erase but enhance the unpredictability of what happens. Through technics, scientific prediction nowadays guides all human existence on earth.

5

The era of the evocation and the era of the destruction of the immutables form the fundamental conflict within Western civilization. But beneath the opposition, both eras are based on the same dimension, namely, the belief in the existence of becoming, in the originary form of the will to power. It is because one believes in the existence and self-evidence of becoming that one evokes the immutable as a remedy against the threat of becoming. And it is because one believes in the existence and self-evidence of becoming that they are destroyed when one realizes that they make becoming impossible.

The belief in becoming is what is common in the two fundamental conflicting epochs of the West. The entire history of the West grows within this belief.

Since the faith in the existence of becoming first comes to light through the philosophical thought of the Ancient Greeks, one can ask – reformulating a famous thesis by Marx – how it is possible that the philosophical *consciousness* of the Ancient Greeks determines the entire *life* of the West. 'It is not consciousness that determines life, but life that determines consciousness', writes Marx. Yet, it is not a matter of overturning Marx's thesis: whether life determines consciousness or consciousness determines life, these two theses share the concept of 'determination', that is, an *action* that makes something pass from nothing to being, and vice versa. Thus, the notion of 'determination' takes shape within the faith in the oscillation of beings between being and nothingness. By stating that this faith is the dimension in which the entire history of the West grows, I do not mean to state that this history is 'determined' by that faith. In the present context, the very words 'growth' and 'history' have a different meaning from the one they have within the essential faith of the West. Within this faith, 'growth' and 'history' are forms of the oscillation between being and nothingness. To speak of the West as the 'history' of nihilism means testifying to the place that has always been, and will always be, open outside the West (and the East, which is simply the prehistory of the West) – the place where the succession of events, and thus the epochs of the West, appear to have a vastly different meaning from the way in which the West understands becoming. The West 'grows' within the faith in the oscillation of beings, in the sense that this faith is the background present in all the events that form Western civilization. After all, this civilization is precisely defined as the set of events that share this background and gradually manifest together with this background.

On the other hand, if for Marx it is human life that determines consciousness (and all cultural and ideological forms), Marx defines human life with the categories that are proper to the Ancient Greek meaning of the oscillation of beings. The 'general nature' of labour is the 'eternal natural condition of human life' (*Capital*, Chapter I, v, 1) and is 'equally common to all forms of human social life'. In Marx's intentions, this is more fundamental than any ideological superstructure. In its 'general nature', labour is a teleological activity that produces 'use values', i.e. things that are useful to humans. The production of 'things' 'detaches' them from the 'immediate nexus' in which they find themselves, that is, it gives 'existence' to what, without labour, does not exist (in a similar way to what happens in the activity of nature). This means that, in its 'general nature', i.e. as the 'eternal natural condition', labour is the activity that makes things oscillate between being and nothingness. (Not in the sense that, when a fish is detached from its immediate nexus with water, before this detachment nothing exists – indeed, the fish in the water pre-exists the fish as a use value, i.e. as ready for cooking; but in the sense that one can state that the use value is produced by labour only if something of it was nothing.) Hence, life, which for Marx should determine every form of consciousness and ideological superstructure, is conceived by Marx according to the categories that are proper to the Ancient Greek consciousness of becoming. According to Marx, life is the foundation of every ideological superstructure; yet the ideology of all ideologies of the West – that is, the Ancient Greek consciousness of the oscillation of beings – is the dimension within which the meaning of life and the 'general nature' of labour, that is, what should be the 'eternal natural condition' of human life, is established.

The immense multiplicity of events forming Western civilization grows within the meaning that the 'thing' has for the Ancient Greeks, because the meaning of being a thing ['dell'esser cosa', t/n] is present in every determinate thing, and because the meaning is not only the content of thought, but also guides and establishes the way one acts. If the meaning of being a fish guides and establishes the actions of the fisherman, and the meaning of being a tree guides and establishes the actions of the woodcutter, the meaning of being a thing is present in the meaning of the fish, of the tree and of everything. Therefore, the meaning of being a thing guides and establishes all action. If the meaning of being a thing changes, all action changes. If in a historical era a certain meaning of being a thing dominates, all action of that era is guided and established by this meaning. The Ancient Greek meaning of being a thing – that is, the 'thing' understood as what oscillates between being and nothingness – is found in all forms of European civilization. That is to say that all European actions are guided and established by the Ancient Greek meaning of the thing. This is the background against which not only all thoughts, but even all European actions stand out. By now, this is the background of the entire Western civilization, that is, the civilization that dominates the planet. It is no longer just the philosopher who looks at 'life' with Ancient Greek eyes, but it is 'life' itself – that is, 'labour', the actions of the masses, the peoples, the institutions – that looks with Ancient Greek eyes. That is to say, it sees everywhere the Ancient Greek meaning of the thing.

Today, in philosophy, there is much talk about the 'linguistic turn': The philosophy of language and hermeneutics are compared to ontology (and to the philosophy of consciousness). Undoubtedly, the things of the world manifest themselves as connected to language and thus as interpretations. But (apart from the 'fact' that in interpreting it is always necessary that there be something to be interpreted, which does not itself appear as an interpretation of anything), this simply means that the structure of things – i.e. by now, of beings – is more complex than traditional thought assumed. Even when one acknowledges that the objects of the world are interpretations, and not pure 'data' existing independently of any theoretical–linguistic–interpretative form, one should still acknowledge that interpretations and languages are not nothing but beings ['non sono un niente, ma sono enti', t/n]. And contemporary thought continues to understand the being of beings (the being a thing ['l'esser cosa', t/n] of things) through the lens of the Ancient Greek meaning of the thing: precisely as that which forces and actions make oscillate between being and nothingness. And this is an oscillation to which also the forces and actions that are believed to determine it belong. In other words, the opposition between hermeneutics and ontology attributes to ontology a limited meaning, for ontology is presented as a consideration of one part or one aspect of the transcendental dimension to which Ancient Greek thought has risen. Therefore, such opposition is *internal* to ontology as the understanding of the transcendental dimension of being ['ente', t/n]–where 'being' ['ente', t/n] is the non-linguistic fact, as well as language and interpretation, as well as the 'datum', the function, the passive object and the activity. Ancient Greek ontology may not have anticipated certain types of beings (and may not have known – as much of traditional thought – that the 'things' of the world are interpretations), but the determinations it brings to light refer to every being, that is, to every non-nothing ['ogni non-niente', t/n], to the transcendental meaning of non-nothing. And it is this meaning that forms the ground on which the entire history of the West develops.

6

Yet the Ancient Greek meaning of the thing – the persuasion that beings emerge from nothingness and return to it – is a testimony of extreme alienation, of the utmost distance from truth. Nonetheless, truth is not something that someone can reach and communicate to others who in turn may come to it. The human being is what the will to power believes it sees when it watches itself. Yet dialogue between human beings is always a misunderstanding. This 'dialogue' is the mask of the struggle between humans. If there exists a 'mutual understanding' between humans, it is the mutual understanding of truth itself. In addition, wherever the world appears, there truth appears. Thus, the extreme distance of truth is not the absence of truth, but the strife between the appearing of truth and the appearing of the persuasion that the world is the dimension where things come out of nothingness and return to it: the strife where what dominates is not the testimony of truth, but the testimony of the persuasion that beings comes out of, and returns to, nothingness. The language that testifies to truth does not lead truth into appearing – truth is always already appearing ['la verità è già da sempre nell'apparire', t/n] –, but it can accompany the twilight of the persuasion that things oscillate between being and nothingness.

A house has been built. The inhabitants of the West think that before the house is built, there already exist the stones, the wood, the land, the design, etc. In other words, they think that before the construction, many elements of the house already exist; but they also think that the *entirety* of what the house is when its construction is complete did *not* pre-exist. They think that what does not exist prior to the construction of the house is the specific unification of materials, the specific unification thanks to which this house is this house. After all, if before the construction of the house *all*, which the house is once the house is built, had already existed, the inhabitants of the West would not say that the house had been built. According to them, the house is built because the specific *unity* of the materials of which the house consists was nothing; and for them, the house is destroyed because such unity returns to nothingness.

However, this unity is a being, that is, it is a non-nothing. By believing that beings – for example, a house – come out of nothingness and return to it, the West believes that there is a time (the past) in which beings were nothing, and a time (the future) in which beings will be nothing. If the inhabitants of the West were told that there exists a time in which the circle was square and a time in which the circle will again be square, they would immediately respond that such a time does not exist because the circle cannot be square. Nevertheless, this sensitivity to the impossible and to contradiction remains completely dormant when they believe that there is a time in which beings, that is, the non-nothing, are nothing. And yet, to believe that beings come from nothingness and return to it means to believe that there is a time in which beings are nothing; and to believe that there is a time in which beings are nothing means to believe that *beings are nothing*. In its essential meaning, nihilism is the persuasion that *things* – human beings, plants, waters, stars, sky, earth, thoughts, feelings, sounds, shapes, cities – *are nothing*: precisely because it is the persuasion that things come from nothingness and return to it. The persuasion that beings are nothing is extreme folly. The West is the history of nihilism because it is the history of the faith that beings oscillate between being and nothingness.

Outside nihilism, truth is the appearing of the eternity of every being – of every thing, gesture, instant, nuance, situation. Outside nihilism, the birth of beings is the appearing and disappearing of the eternal. But here it is of interest to conclude by stating that, exactly because the faith in the oscillation of beings between being and nothingness is extreme folly, the extreme error, such faith believes that the impossible exists. The will to power wants the Impossible. Even the most tender and delicate act of will wants the Impossible. No technics ['tecnica', t/n], divine or human, can bring anything out of nothingness or annihilate even the most irrelevant and shadowy of things. Even the most irrelevant and shadowy of beings is eternal, just as the very extreme folly of nihilism is eternal. As the extreme form of the will to power, the West is extreme impotence. The spectacles of creative and destructive violence, which culminate in Western civilization, do not show, do not manifest the process of coming out of nothing and the annihilation of things (nihilism is also a nihilistic interpretation of appearing and of experience). Rather, they show what the eternals are that appear when the folly of the will to power believes to dominate the world. Yet it is possible that these spectacles may come to set – that is, that their appearing may reach its completion. And it is possible that the West may come to set and a different path from the one, along which the West walks, may enter into appearing.

NOTES

Foreword

1 *La tendenza fondamentale del nostro tempo*, Milano, Adelphi, 1988; second edition 2008.

2 Severino, Emanuele, *Essenza del nichilismo*, Milan, Adelphi, 1982; Egl.tr. The essence of nihilism, edited by Ines Testoni and Alessandro Carrera, New York, Verso, 2015.

3 Severino, Emanuele, *Oltre il linguaggio*, Milano, Adelphi, 1992; Engl. tr. *Beyond Language*, translated by Damiano Sacco, edited by Ines Testoni, Damiano Sacco and Giulio Goggi, London, Bloomsbury, 2023

4 Severino, Emanuele, *La struttura originaria*, Brescia, La Scuola, 1958-2014; New edition, Milano, Adelphi, 1981.

5 Severino, Emanuele, *Legge e caso*, Milan, Adelphi, 1978; Engl. tr. *Law and chance*, translated by Damiano Sacco, edited by Ines Testoni, Damiano Sacco and Giulio Goggi, London, Bloomsbury, 2022.

6 Severino, Emanuele, *Téchne. Le radici della violenza*, Milan, Rusconi, 1979; second ed., 1988; new expanded edition, Milan, Rizzoli, 2002; *Law and chance*, Milan, Adelphi, 1979; La filosofia futura, Milan, Rizzoli, 1989; new expanded edition, 2005; *Il destino della tecnica*, Milan, Rizzoli, 1998; new edition, 2009; Democrazia, tecnica, capitalismo, Brescia, Morcelliana, 2009.

'In technology we trust'

1 Cf. Severino, Emanuele. *La tendenza fondamentale del nostro tempo*. Milan: Adelphi, 1988. For an wide-ranging overview of Severino's philosophy, cf. Goggi, Giulio. *Emanuele Severino*. Vatican City: Lateran University Press, 2015; and Cusano, Nicoletta. *Emanuele Severino: Oltre il nichilismo*. Brescia: Morcelliana, 2011.

2 This definition is taken from the *Cambridge Dictionary* [online], accessed on the 30 October 2024.

3 This second definition is itself taken from the online *Cambridge Dictionary* [online] accessed 30 October 2024.

4 Cf. Chapter 7 in this book.

5 Cf. Severino's *Introduction* in this book. Cf. also Chapter 5, section 5, and Chapter 7.

6 For Severino's judgement of the Western culture as the extreme alienation, cf. Chapter 7.

7 Cf. the present translation. As examples, cf. Chapter 5, section 5, and Chapter 7.

8 Cf. this book, for instance Chapter 2, sections 9 and 10.

9 Everything that Severino says with regards to the nothingness of the future can be repeated about the nothingness of the past. However, following Severino's own tendency in this book, I leave aside the entification of the past, for it is analogous to the entification of the future.

10 Cf. this book, Chapter 7, section 4. Let me mention that Severino has devoted three monographic studies to the philosophy of Giacomo Leopardi, who is by him considered the first 'destroyer' ('distruttore') of Western (traditional) metaphysics. Let me quote those studies: Severino, Emanuele. *Il nulla e la poesia*. Milan: BUR Rizzoli, 2021; Severino, Emanuele. *Cosa arcana e stupenda*. Milan: BUR Rizzoli, 2006; Severino, Emanuele. *In viaggio con Leopardi: La partita sul destino dell'uomo*. Milan: BUR Rizzoli, 2015.

11 Cf. Chapter 7, section 4.

12 Cf. Severino, Emanuele. *Beyond Language*, transl. by Damiano Sacco, ed. by Giulio Goggi, Damiano Sacco, and Ines Testoni. London: Bloomsbury Academic, 2023; and Severino, Emanuele. *Law and Chance*, transl. Damiano Sacco, ed. Giulio Goggi, Damiano Sacco, and Iines Testoni. London: Bloomsbury Academic, 2023.

13 I should mention that I have further developed these considerations in Lucarelli, Antimo. 'Is Metaphysics Totalitarian? First Remarks on Politics and Metaphysics in Emanuele Severino', in *Italian Thought*, ed. F. Dal Bo and C. Salzani (New York: SUNY Press, 2025, pp. 97–117). For a more general philosophical conversation with Heidegger and Severino, cf. Lucarelli, Antimo. *Per un nuovo concetto di fenomeno: Muovendo da Heidegger e Severino* (Soveria Mannelli: Rubbettino, 2021).

14 Let me mention that Severino introduces the notion of 'alienation' at the end of *The Fundamental Tendency of Our Time*, in Chapter 7, as a reference to his writings concerning the 'destiny of necessity' ('destino della necessità'), that is, the 'originary structure' ('struttura originaria'). Those are the names given by Severino to the 'incontrovertible truth' ('verità incontrovertibile'): This truth, however, lies on 'a different path from the one, along which the West walks' ('un sentiero diverso da quello lungo il quale l'Occidente cammina') (Chapter 7, section 6).

15 Cf. this book, Chapter 2, section 6 as an example.

16 The meaning of this technological 'destination' ('destinazione') of all forces is not marked by any determinism. Yet this is not directly relevant for the purposes of this introduction. Therefore, the reader can refer to the translation below. Cf. for instance Chapter 2, section 12.

17 Cf. Chapter 6, section 1. Cf. also Chapter 3, section 1.

18 Cf. section 6.

19 Cf. Chapter 6.

Chapter 2

1 It is true that the contradiction between the scientific–technological organization and the ideological organization of existence actualizes in the situation (that is, in the contradiction) where ideology, even pursuing the peculiar goal of the scientific–technological Apparatus – namely, the indefinite increase in power, to which ideology subordinates its own goals – nonetheless continues, contradictorily, to treat this increase as a means in relation to the ideological purpose it aims for (for instance, the realization of socialism, the defence of economic freedoms, the promotion of Christian values). But it is also true that an ideology could free itself from this contradiction by deciding to pursue the increase in power only up to the point beyond which this would imply the subordination of the ideological end to the technological end. (This is an intention that all ideologies claim to have, yet it is proving extremely difficult to identify the location of that limiting point, as demonstrated, for example, by the relationships between Catholic doctrine and science or between Soviet Marxism and science.) In any case, the fundamental tendency currently underway on the planet is the progressive disappearance of the attitude that utilizes the indefinite increase in power as a means for achieving an ideological end.

2 The 'Report' commissioned by the Club of Rome does not deny that the Apparatus is dominating the world; it denies that, given the way in which the Apparatus is dominating, such dominance may have a long life. Regardless of the imbalances in this 'Report', which critics have underscored on various fronts, it should be noted that the trends leading to the collapse of the system, within the system's variables, are all of an ideological kind. That is, such trends represent the development of the ideological arrangement of existence: The rejection of birth control is ideological (i.e. attributable to ethnoreligious traditions); the will to maintain industrial structures that do not employ alternative energy, worsen planetary pollution, and overlook technologies capable of increasing food availability is ideological (i.e. such a will expresses a defence of established economic interests). From the standpoint of the 'Report' itself, it appears that the system tends towards collapse not because

the Apparatus itself tends toward collapse, but because the functioning of the Apparatus is hindered by the traditional forms in which the Apparatus currently lies. Even the clash between rich and poor countries is a contradiction in relation to the unity formed by the totality of human purposes. And the prediction that the rich will act so as to avoid the collapse foreseen by the 'Report' is a mere conjecture, i.e. the hypothesis that this contradiction will be solved by the prevalence of wealthy countries. Yet, even in this case, the conjecture is not irrefutable self-evidence that this is the direction towards which the contradiction is to be solved.

3   Cf. Severino, Emanuele. *Interpretazione e traduzione dell'Orestea di Eschilo*. Milan, Rizzoli, 1985.

4   Severino distinguishes between 'being' ('l'essere') and 'beings' ('gli enti', 'gli essenti'). I always translate 'l'essere' with 'being', but I do not always translate 'l'ente' and 'l'essente' (singular forms of 'gli enti', 'gli essenti') with 'beings', though I do that in most cases. The cases where I do not translate 'l'ente' (or 'l'essente') with 'beings' are (1) when I translate 'l'ente' with 'a being'; (2) when Severino speaks of 'il senso greco dell'ente': In that case, I translate with 'the Ancient Greek meaning of *being*', as it would be unsatisfactory to translate with 'the ancient Greek meaning of beings' or 'the ancient Greek meaning of a being'. [T/n].

5   Cf. Severino, Emanuele. *Gli abitatori del tempo*. Rome, Armando, 1978, Chapter III; and Severino, Emanuele. *Destino della necessità*. Milan, Adelphi, 1980, Chapter II.

6   Cf. Severino, Emanuele. *Law and Chance*, transl. by Damiano Sacco, ed. by Giulio Goggi, Damiano Sacco, and Ines Testoni. London, Bloomsbury, 2023. [T/n]

Chapter 3

1   Cf. Severino, Emanuele. *Law and chance*, op. cit., p. 53 et seq.; and Severino, Emanuele. *Destino della Necessità*, cit., Chapter XV.

Chapter 4

1   Cf. Severino, Emanuele. *The Originary Structure*, trans. Damiano Sacco, ed. Giulio Goggi, Damiano Sacco, and Ines Testoni. London, Bloomsbury, 2025. [T/n].

2   Cf. also Severino, Emanuele. *The Essence of Nihilism*, transl. Giacomo Donis, ed. Ines Testoni and Alessandro Carrera. London, Verso 2016, pp. 59–80 (Italian edition: Severino, Emanuele. *Essenza del Nichilismo*. Milan, Adelphi, 1982). [Severino also

quotes, here, pp. 116–133 of the Italian edition, consisting of a concluding *Note* to the *Postscript* to *Returning to Parmenides*. These pages, however, have not been incorporated into the English translation. T/n].

3   English translations from Aristotle's *Metaphysics* are taken from Aristotle. *Metaphysics: A Revised Text With Introduction and Commentary*, ed. and trans. W. D. Ross. Oxford, Oxford University Press, 1924. I should mention, however, that Severino uses in this book his own translations of Aristotle's text, often explicating what he feels is implicit in the Aristotelian text. Nonetheless, I have avoided translating Severino's own translation. I have rather chosen to quote Ross' translation. [T/n].

4   I am quoting from the Popper, Karl R. *The Open Society and Its* Enemies, Vol. 2: Hegel, Marx, and the Aftermath. St. Paul, Minn, 1971 (the emphasis in the English translation is slightly different). [T/n].

5   I am quoting from the English edition Habermas, Jurgen. *Moral Consciousness and Communicative Action*, ed. and trans. Christian Lenhardt and Shierry W. Nicholsen. Cambridge, MIT University Press, 1990, pp. 88–9.[T/n].

6   I am quoting from Popper, Karl R. *Conjectures and Refutations: The Growth of Scientific Knowledge*. London, New York, Basic Books, 1963, p. 387. [T/n].

7   Emphasis in original. [T/n]

8   Cf. Emanuele Severino. *Studi di filosofia della prassi*, 1962; second edition, Milan Adelphi, 1984, part I, Chapter II, p. 6.

9   Severino, Emanuele. *The Essence of Nihilism*, op. cit., 'Aletheia' (pp. 313–34) and 'The Earth and the essence of man', section VI, pp. 219 et seq.; and before that, cf. Severino, Emanuele. *Studi di filosofia della prassi*, op. cit., footnote on p. 181.

Chapter 5

1   Cf. Severino, Emanuele. *Destino della necessità*, op. cit., Chapter VII, sections 5–6; Chapter XI, section 1.

2   In this passage, I have translated Severino's own translation of Plato, because otherwise what Severino is meaning here would be lost. On the other hand, Benjamin Jowett's translation of Plato (Plato. *The Dialogues of Plato*, 4 vols, trans. by B. Jowett. Oxford, Clarendon Press, 1953) contains 'poetry or making' rather than 'production' (the word used by Plato is *poiesis*), 'art' instead of 'technique' (the Ancient Greek word is *techne*). Moreover, Jowett's translation does not contain the word 'cause' (*aitia*) and therefore reads: 'All creation or passage of nonbeing into being is poetry or making'. [T/n].

Chapter 6

1. In contemporary Italian, 'indótto' (with a closed 'o') is the past participle of the verb 'indurre' (English: 'to induce'). On the other hand, 'indòtto' (with an open 'o') is an adjective alluding to someone's lack of erudition. [T/n].

2. I think Severino meant to say '50 per cent + 1' of the votes. [T/n].

3. In relation to these considerations, which I have been developing for some time (see my essays Severino, Emanuele. *Téchne*. Milan, Rusconi, 1979; and Severino Emanuele. *A Cesare e a Dio*. Milan, Rizzoli, 1983), it has been argued that one cannot 'put on the same level' liberal democracy and Eastern communism, and the freedoms enjoyed under a democratic regime have been listed (L. Pellicani, 'Corriere della Sera', 17 October 1984). I was aware of these freedoms too. Moreover, I have never intended to argue that there are not well-known differences between the two antagonistic political systems. Nonetheless, the question remains as to whether Western democracies are simply a mechanism that registers the will of the majority, wherever this will may lead, or if they are a mechanism that, in addition to registering, acts effectively to prevent communist and pro-Soviet forces from coming to power. Do they merely stand by, prepared to raise the red flag if the majority were to vote for it? Do they simply oppose communism using the tools of democratic legality? Is this legality truly the dominant and ultimately decisive force in Western countries? An affirmative answer to this question would be perplexing. Just as it would be perplexing to hear that robust, adult persons would not react in any fashion if they were slapped. Just as one can say that robust, adult persons 'do not tolerate, in fact as a matter of principle' being slapped by those to whom they could respond in kind, one can also say that Western democracies 'exclude, in fact as a matter of principle, that power can be seized by communist and pro-Soviet forces'. It has been conceded to me that Western democracies 'deny that power can be handed over to anti-system parties'; but it is also noted that 'no anti-system party has won the majority of votes in a Western country'. Agreed; but the point to explain is how Western democracies 'deny' that power can be taken by anti-system forces. Precisely, I am saying that this 'denial' is not a simple mental operation of someone standing by, disapproving of the behaviour of a group of passersby. Bobbio speaks precisely of 'invisible power'. Yet – even if it may be a bitter pill – I would add that it would be surprising if this power did not exist. Real democracy is inseparable from real capitalism, and the survival instinct of the latter excludes, as a matter of principle, that the democratic principle of respecting the majority's will should be fully applied to the point where the majority's will is to overthrow the capitalist system.

4. 'The road' (Italian: 'la strada') does not occur in the original text. Nonetheless, I think Severino meant to say that '*the road* to hell is paved with good intentions', as in the corresponding Italian saying ('la strada per l'inferno è lastricata di buone intenzioni'). [T/n].

5   Therefore, one cannot object that my thesis on the social democratization of the PCI entails an excessively 'voluntaristic' conception of this party's actions (P. Ingrao, *Tradizione e Progetto*. Bari, De Donato, p. 113). If anything, the 'destiny' I allude to could be misunderstood as 'fatalism' or 'determinism'. But even in such a second case, this would be a misunderstanding, because all fatalisms and determinisms belong to the same essence as voluntarism, namely, to the Ancient Greek faith in becoming. This faith includes *both* the evocation of the immutable, as present in 'determinism' and 'fatalism' as statements of a rule from which becoming cannot deviate, and the destruction of the immutable, which frees becoming from any 'predetermined' framework or 'fatal' course, establishing free will as the sole principle of human development.

6   On the distinction between 'contradictoriness' and 'contradicting oneself', see Severino, Emanuele. *The Originary Structure, op. cit.*, Chapter VIII; and *The Essence of Nihilism, op. cit.*, pp. 217–31, and 323–33. For the relationship between that distinction and Marxism, see Severino, Emanuele. *Gli Abitatori del Tempo, op. cit.*, Chapter 2; and Severino, Emanuele. *Téchne, op. cit.*, Chapter III, section 4; and Severino, Emanuele. *A Cesare e a Dio, op. cit.*, Chapter XII.

7   The essay *Discorso sull'economia politica* (Turin, Boringhieri, 1985) by Claudio Napoleoni addresses these two opposite criticisms, which rely respectively on Sraffa and on Kelsen and Popper. Napoleoni offers an in grand style economic discourse, which develops towards the fundamental philosophical problems of our time. Napoleoni's surprising thesis is that the essential core of Sraffa's thought pushes towards a reformulation of both Marxian and neoclassical theory, and that once reformulated, they are no longer antagonistic but complementary. Therefore, Napoleoni clears the field of the incongruous criticisms directed at the two theories, dismantling the anti-capitalist interpretation of Sraffa and showing the inconsistency of the criticism made by Popper and Kelsen of Marx's dialectics as a denial of the principle of non-contradiction. Because in Italy the Popper–Kelsen was repeated by L. Colletti, and because I had shown its groundlessness at that time (cf. Severino, Emanuele. *Gli abitatori del tempo, op. cit.*, Chapter II), Napoleoni draws on my criticism of how Colletti attempts to rid himself of Marx.

8   Colletti's mistake (and the mistake of many others) lies in believing that, in Hegel and Marx, the unity and relationship between opposites means the cancellation of their opposition, and that therefore Hegelian reason is the most flagrant violation of the principle of non-contradiction. Napoleoni mentions a passage where Colletti, in response to me, invites reflection on the fact that for Hegel the unity ['l'unione', t/n] of opposites (in Hegel's words themselves) 'contains a contradiction'. For Colletti, this would demonstrate that the unity of opposites for Hegel is a negation of the principle of non-contradiction. In addition to what Napoleoni writes on this, I would add that Colletti interprets this sentence of Hegel as if Hegel were saying that the unity of opposites *is* a contradiction. On the contrary, Hegel says that this unity 'contains' a contradiction. And he is right. Indeed, the principle of non-contradiction (i.e. the denial that contradiction exists in reality) 'contains' the contradiction; it contains

it precisely as *that which is negated*. Or, put another way: the negation that good is evil contains the assertion that good is evil; but again, it contains it *as negated*. Therefore, even that sentence of Hegel, and all similar sentences, cannot be used to document Hegel and Marx's opposition to the concrete meaning of the principle of non-contradiction. However, does Hegel not affirm that 'all things are in themselves contradictory' (*The Science of Logic*, Vol. II, Section I, Chapter II, C, Note 3)? Of course! But in that context, Hegel is alluding to 'finite things', that is inadequately thought things, while authentic thinking ['il pensiero autentico', t/n] – as he writes – does not 'succumb to contradiction', nor 'allows itself to be dominated' by it. Rather, it *negates* it. And in this sense, it 'contains' it.

9   Napoleoni is well aware that the kind of criticism to be directed, in my opinion, at Marx, Hegel, and at philosophy in general is quite different. Thus, he offers me a series of provocations that essentially regard the possibility of keeping Marx alive within certain fundamental structures of my discourse. Yet, Napoleoni is also receptive to Heidegger, who believes that Marx's demand to liberate humanity from alienation by restoring its productive capacity and control over the world inevitably pushes towards transforming the human being itself into a product of the productive apparatus. Except that even Heidegger thinks that the productivity of humans and their control over the world are real. It seems to me that Napoleoni shares my thesis that the true form of alienation lies precisely in believing in the reality itself of domination – while, in fact, domination is something that emerges within the intention, that is, within the dream that domination is real. It emerges within the faith in becoming. In the meantime, one might ask Heidegger: Why cannot the human being be a product? What is there in him which is so untouchable that one must refrain from treating him as just another product? This question needs to be answered, unless one wants the defence of humanity to be reduced to a simple subjective demand – precisely that 'demand' or 'subjectivity' which is at the root of the productive process, where even the human being becomes a product.

10 In this and in similar cases, Severino quotes passages from a text which he does not reference in his book. In all these cases, I do not reference the text either, as this lack of an explicit quotation belongs to Severino's quotation style. [T/n].

11 Cf. Corriere della Sera, 15 Settembre 1985.

REFERENCES

Aristotle (1924). *Metaphysics: A Revised Text With Introduction and Commentary*, ed. and transl. by W. D. Ross. Oxford: Oxford University Press.
Cambridge Dictionary [online].
Cusano, N. (2011). *Emanuele Severino. Oltre il nichilismo*. Brescia: Morcelliana.
Goggi, G. (2015). *Emanuele Severino*. Vatican City: Lateran University Press.
Habermas, J. (1990). *Moral Consciousness and Communicative Action*, ed. and transl. by C. Lenhardt and S. W. Nicholsen. Cambridge: MIT University Press.
Ingrao, P. (1982). *Tradizione e Progetto*. Bari: De Donato.
Lucarelli, A. (2021). *Per un nuovo concetto di fenomeno: Muovendo da Heidegger e Severino*. Soveria Mannelli: Rubbettino.
Lucarelli, A. (2025). 'Is metaphysics totalitarian? First remarks on politics and metaphysics in Emanuele Severino'. In *Italian Thought*, ed. F. Dal Bo and C. Salzani. New York: SUNY Press, pp. 97–117.
Napoleoni, C. (1985). *Discorso sull'economia politica*, Turin: Boringhieri.
Pellicani, L. (1984). 'Corriere della Sera', October 17.
Plato (1953). *The Dialogues of Plato*, 4 vols, trans. by B. Jowett. Oxford: Clarendon Press.
Popper, K. R. (1963). *Conjectures and Refutations: The Growth of Scientific Knowledge*. London: Basic Books.
Popper, K. R. (1971). *The Open Society and Its Enemies, Vol. 2: Hegel, Marx, and the Aftermath*. St. Paul, Minn: Princeton University Press.
Severino, E. (1962). *Studi di filosofia della prassi*; 2nd edition (1984), Milan: Adelphi.
Severino, E. (1978). *Gli abitatori del tempo*. Rome: Armando.
Severino, E. (1979). *Téchne*. Milan: Rusconi.
Severino, E. (1980). *Destino della necessità. Κατὰ τὸ χρεών*. Milan: Adelphi.
Severino, E. (1981). *La struttura originaria*. Milan: Adelphi.
Severino, E. (1983). *A Cesare e a Dio*. Milan: Rizzoli.
Severino, E. (1985). *Interpretazione e traduzione dell'Orestea di Eschilo*. Milan: Rizzoli.
Severino, E. (1988). *La tendenza fondamentale del nostro tempo*. Milan: Adelphi.
Severino, E. (2006). *Cosa arcana e stupenda*. Milan: BUR Rizzoli.
Severino, E. (2015). *In viaggio con Leopardi: La partita sul destino dell'uomo*. Milan: BUR Rizzoli.
Severino, E. (2016). *The Essence of Nihilism*, trans. by G. Donis, ed. by I. Testoni and A. Carrera. London: Verso.
Severino, E. (2021). *Il nulla e la poesia*. Milan: BUR Rizzoli.
Severino, E. (2023). *Beyond Language*, trans. by D. Sacco, ed. by G. Goggi, D. Sacco, and I. Testoni. London: Bloomsbury Academic.
Severino, E. (2023). *Law and Chance*, trans. by D. Sacco, ed. by G. Goggi, D. Sacco, and I. Testoni. London: Bloomsbury Academic.
Severino, E. (2025). *The Originary Structure*, trans. by D. Sacco, ed. by G. Goggi, D. Sacco, and I. Testoni. London: Bloomsbury Academic.

INDEX

A Cesare e a Dio (Severino) 178–9
action 28, 30, 43, 48, 64, 71, 78–9, 83–4, 90, 96, 98–9, 110, 114–16, 117–22, 150, 159, 167–170, 177
actual appearing 103
alienation 50, 128, 157, 170, 180
Ancient Greek ontology 68, 127, 164, 170
Ancient Greek philosophy 25–26, 63, 67, 85–86, 118, 155–6, 158–9, 161, 163
annihilation 27, 30, 48, 172
Apel, K. O. 90, 92, 94, 96–8
aporia 91, 153
Aristotle 91–2, 94, 100–3, 105–7, 153, 156

becoming 28–30, 34, 45, 53, 60–5, 68–9, 84–7, 104–5, 112, 116–25, 127–9, 156–61, 163–8, 179
beings 101, 105–7, 122, 127, 155–8, 160–4, 166–172
being a thing 168–9
beings, *qua* beings 156–8
Bernstein, E. 145
Brahmana of a Hundred Paths 77

capacity to achieve purposes 47
Capital (Marx) 151
capitalism 38–9, 46, 57, 72–4, 111–12, 118, 122, 124, 132, 135, 138–41, 145–6, 149–52, 158, 162, 178
Catholicism 57
Christ 77, 82
Christianity 29, 46, 72–3, 118, 124, 143, 159, 164–5
civilization of technics 27, 29, 36, 41–4, 50, 54, 57–8, 69, 110, 118–19, 122, 128, 159–60
cogito ergo sum 92
collapse 33, 37, 41, 54–5, 93, 175–6

Colletti, L. 179
coming from nothingness 28, 66, 165
common sense 62, 97, 141
Conjectures and Refutations (Popper) 93, 95
(non-) contradiction 48, 52–5, 57–8, 64, 68–9, 91–4, 98–100, 102–3, 106–7, 114, 120, 125, 132, 141, 144–53, 158, 165, 171, 175–6, 179–80
Convivium (Plato) 116
coquetry 150–2
creative destruction 39, 57

Day of Judgment 77
decision(s) 78, 81–3, 94, 140–1
demiourgos (or demiurge) 76, 116, 160
democracy 46, 73, 134–5, 138, 140–8, 178
Descartes, René 92
destination 63, 68–9, 125, 128, 143
Destino della Necessità (Severino) 123, 128
destiny 113, 125, 128, 141, 143, 148, 179
destruction 26–8, 30, 38–42, 48–9, 52, 55, 57, 64, 86, 89, 118, 128, 137, 163–6, 179–80
determinacy 101–2, 104–6
determination(s) 39, 90–1, 100–1, 119–20, 124–5, 127–28, 141, 167, 170
Discorso sull'Economia Politica (Napoleoni) 179
domination 28–30, 35, 38, 53, 62, 65–6, 68–9, 71–3, 76–7, 79–81, 83–4, 110, 117, 121–2, 132, 160, 163, 165, 180
Duumvirate 25–6, 111, 113–14

Earth 25, 29–30, 35–9, 46, 52, 55–6, 63, 74, 79–81, 110, 114, 117, 125–6, 133, 139, 157, 166, 172, 177
Einaudi, Luigi 112

élenchos 89–92, 94, 101–4, 106
entification 61–2, 89, 119, 125
epamphoterízein 116, 155
erring 147, 153
error 33, 44, 106, 147, 152
eternal 28, 106, 121, 128, 156, 163, 168, 172
eternal forms 28
ethics of science 71–4, 84–5, 87, 90
Europe 25–6, 29–31, 109–16, 120, 122–4, 129, 157, 163–4
experimental method 65, 166

faith 28–31, 35, 42–3, 51, 58, 60, 62, 69, 76–87, 89, 93–4, 96, 98, 103, 105, 110, 113, 118–25, 128–9, 141–2, 159–60, 162–3, 167, 172, 179–80
Freud, Sigmund 50, 147
future, the 46, 55, 58, 61–9, 171

Gedankenformen 151
Gentile, Giovanni 97
Gli Abitatori del Tempo (Severino) 179
God(s) 30, 58, 61, 76–7, 141, 156, 160, 162

Habermas, Jürgen 92, 94–100
Hegel, Georg Wilhelm Friedrich 53, 96, 115, 145, 148–50, 157–8, 177, 179–80
Heidegger, Martin 43, 122, 157, 160, 180
hermeneutic philosophy 96
Hilferding, R. 145
Hintikka, J. 93
History and Class Consciousness (Lukács) 144
Hobbes, Thomas 112–13
Hopkins Sheila V. 40
human being(s) 28, 30, 42–5, 48–9, 77, 94, 119, 165, 170, 172, 180
humanism 29, 49, 72
hypothetical 55, 83, 95–96, 103–4, 166

ideological 41, 47–9, 51–2, 56–7, 63, 114, 167–9, 175–6
impotence 43, 51, 172
incontrovertible truth(s) 35, 42, 75, 81–2, 119, 142, 164

indefinite increase 48, 63, 74, 175
infinite increase 73, 75
Ingrao, P. 179
interpretation 28, 54, 56, 78, 81–2, 86–7, 90, 95–6, 101, 103, 128, 139, 164, 160–70, 172
isolation 109–10, 114–16, 117–19, 121–3, 125, 127–9
Italian Communist Party 57, 111, 132, 134
Italy 57, 131–140, 179
Introduction to Psychoanalysis (Freud) 147

Kant, Immanuel 52, 92, 95–6, 148
Kelsen, H. 146–9, 152, 179
Keynes, J. M. 39

laws of 'truth' 61
limit 28–9, 44, 73, 90, 114, 126, 160
listener 61
Luhmann, N. 125, 147
Lukács, György 144–6, 152

Mann, Thomas 140
Marx, K. 39, 46, 53, 56–7, 107, 118–19, 122–4, 143–52, 158, 167–8, 175, 177, 179–80
Mead, G. H. 94
Meadows, D.H. 33–4, 37, 42
Meaning 26, 118–19, 162–4
meaning of being and nothingness 59, 62, 65, 85, 117, 120, 156–60, 168–9, 176
Metaphysics (Aristotle) 91, 103, 106–7, 153
mode of production 56–7
Moral Consciousness and Communicative Action (Habermas) 99
multiplicity 81, 110, 114, 118–20, 124–5, 128–9, 157, 168

Napoleoni, C. 179–80
neofunctionalism 126–7, 147
Neurath, O. 77
Nietzsche, Friedrich Wilhelm 44, 75, 95, 102, 157, 164
nihil absolutum 155

nihilism 104–6, 155, 157–8, 167, 172
nothingness 27–8, 30, 59–69, 85–6, 104, 116–21, 155–66, 168–72, 174
novelty 27, 61, 64, 67

objective fact 76, 78, 81–2, 95
objective spirit 52
observable frequency 53
occurrence 53, 55, 65–8, 147
ontology 68, 85, 127, 164, 169–70
oscillation 60, 62, 116, 118–19, 155–7, 159–64, 166–8, 170, 172

paradox(es) 132, 133–4
Peirce, C. S. 77, 94
Pellicani, L. 178
Peters, R. S. 90, 92–3
Phelps Brown, H. 40
philosophical prediction 26, 75, 115, 118–19, 128, 162–4
philosophy 25–6, 29, 43, 49–50, 61–3, 67, 72, 85–6, 89–90, 96–7, 112, 115, 118, 124, 141, 145, 147–8, 155–6, 158–9, 161, 163, 165, 169, 180
Plato 75, 91–2, 103, 116, 155–7, 160
Popper, Karl 77, 92–8, 146–9, 179
pragmatism 96
prediction(s) 26, 33, 38, 53–5, 59–60, 65–6, 68, 161–3, 165–6, 176
prevision 61–2, 65
pre-ontological 124
principium firmissimum 91, 153
principle of non-contradiction 52, 92–3, 100, 102, 106, 145–50, 152–3, 158, 179–80
probabilistic 53, 55, 143, 166
production 26–30, 33, 39–40, 56–7, 72, 86, 116, 118, 122, 133, 150, 168, 177
Protagoras (Plato) 75

real socialism 39, 46, 72, 131–2, 140–1
refutation 91, 93–4, 95, 103
Republic (Plato) 116, 135, 155
resolution (of contradiction) 68–9, 153
returning to nothingness 28

rhetoric 51
Ricardo, David 148
Robinson Crusoe 77, 80, 99
rules of interpretation 54

sacrifice(s) 77, 79, 82
sayability 91
scepticism 94, 97–98
Schumpeter, J. A. 38–9, 57
science 25–9, 33–7, 45–6, 49–53, 55–6, 58–9, 63, 65–9, 71–87, 89–90, 93, 97, 109–10, 114–15, 116–17, 124, 141, 143–8, 152, 159, 164–6, 175, 180
scientific prediction 26, 55, 65, 68, 166
scientific-technological arrangement 35–6, 63
scientific-technological rationality 43, 46–7, 49–50, 52, 54, 56–7, 60, 62–3, 66, 68
self-contradiction 52, 91–2
self-evidence 42, 61, 85–6, 123–4, 157, 164–6, 176
self-negation 91, 104, 106
Servan-Schreiber 36–7
Simmel, Georg 150
Smith, Adam 148
Sophist (Plato) 91, 160
Soviet Union 25, 26, 46–7, 56, 111–12, 116, 139
Spirito, Ugo 97
Sraffa Piero 148, 179
standing 123, 128, 162
superpower(s) 25, 37–40, 54–5, 111–12, 114, 120, 133
Superstate 25, 39, 112, 115, 133
supersystem 52–3
supreme purpose 47, 72
synthesis 91, 118–19, 122

téchne 160, 177
technics 25–30, 36, 41–4, 48–52, 54, 57–8, 68–9, 71, 74, 89, 110, 116, 118–20, 122, 124, 128, 133, 159–60, 166, 172
technological apparatus 25, 29, 46–9, 53, 55, 64, 66–9, 71–2, 74, 77, 79, 83–5, 90, 110, 114–15, 122, 124–5, 127, 133, 175

technology 45–6
tendency 37, 45, 52–4, 56–7, 63, 68–69, 113, 140, 143, 175
terrorism 131, 134–9
The Essence of Nihilism 104, 106, 153, 176–7, 179
The Open Society and Its Enemies (Popper) 93, 97
The Originary Structure (Severino) 90, 148
the originary structure 91, 104, 106
The Science of Logic (Hegel) 180
thinkability 91
Tradizione e Progetto (Ingrao) 179
twilight 44, 122, 171

unconscious, the 30, 67–8, 147, 158
United States 25, 36, 46–7, 112, 116, 139, 141
unpredictability 59, 65–6, 81, 161–3, 165–6
Übermensch 44

violence 41–2, 63, 100, 121, 139, 142, 172

Warsh, David 40
Watt, A. J. 91–92
Weber Max 35, 112, 138, 142
West 28, 30–31, 43, 57–62, 64, 68–9, 71, 75, 85–6, 89, 104, 115, 121–5, 127–9, 135, 140–1, 155, 157–159, 161–5, 167–8, 171–2, 174
Western tradition 42, 54, 60–4, 68, 122
what-is-to-be-dominated 28–9, 58–60, 68–9, 84, 159
whole, the 61, 67, 116
will for truth 61–3, 65–6, 68–9
will to power 28–31, 48–51, 57–63, 66–9, 73, 75, 79, 84–5, 121, 123, 127, 133, 159–62, 165–6, 170, 172